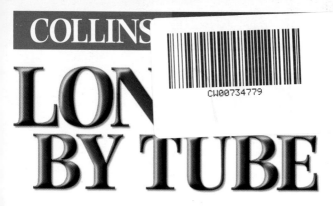

# COLLINS
# LONDON
# BY TUBE

# CONTENTS

HarperCollins*Publishers*

Published by Collins
*An imprint of HarperCollins*Publishers
77-85 Fulham Palace Road, Hammersmith, London W6 8JB

The HarperCollins website address is: www.**fire**and**water**.com

The Collins London by Tube has been created from a concept by M. Godfrey.

Designed and produced by HarperCollins*Publishers* Limited,
Unit 4, Manchester Park, Tewkesbury Road, Cheltenham, GL51 9EJ
Maps and indices © HarperCollinsPublishers Limited 1999
Exit/Entry and concept © M. Godfrey in association with London Underground

Collins® is a registered trademark of HarperCollins*Publishers* Limited

Mapping generated from Bartholomew digital databases

Bartholomew website address is: www.bartholomewmaps.com

Underground Map © and Underground logo ® London Regional Transport
Reg. User No. 99/3098

Printed & bound by Imago in Singapore

ISBN 0 00 449022 3     MM10380     RNN

e-mail: roadcheck@harpercollins.co.uk

# The London Underground

The London Underground system, commonly known as the 'tube', is the simplest way of getting around London and is a particularly efficient way to travel in the area of central London covered by this atlas. There is also a good service to north, east and west London, for example, the Piccadilly line to Heathrow. Some lines run south of the river, in particular the Jubilee line extension to North Greenwich due to be completed in 1999 and the Northern line as far as Morden. There are also good connections to the Docklands Light Railway system (DLR) and National Rail mainline stations.

The tube comprises of twelve separate lines, each colour-coded on the unique 'tube map' (see inside back cover) which makes the system easy to understand and very easy to use.

**The tube runs between approx 05.30-0015 Mon-Sat, 07.30-23.30 Sun.**
All tube stations have a notice showing the times of the first and last trains.
Timetables are issued free at London Travel Information Centres.

**Fares** are graduated according to zones. Travelcards, giving unlimited travel within or across zones can be purchased for a day*, a week, a month or a year and can provide considerable savings. In addition to the Underground, they can also be used on buses, the DLR and rail services in the London area. Travelcards can be bought at any tube station or London Travel Information Centre. To save queuing at ticket offices, keep some 5p, 10p, 20p and £1 coins handy to use in the self-service ticket machines. You must keep your ticket to use in the exit machine when you reach your destination°. When planning a trip on the Underground it is as well to know that the journey time between stations is, on average, about 3 minutes.

**Smoking** is illegal anywhere on the Underground, including in the ticket halls, on stairs, escalators and platforms, as well as on the trains.

## Docklands Light Railway (DLR)

Built in 1987 to serve the Docklands area in East London, this system connects with the Underground system and runs from Bank to Beckton, with an extension to Lewisham due to open during 1999. The trains, in their red, white and blue livery are computer-controlled but do have a guard/ticket-collector on board. The system offers good, high-level views over the stretches of water which form the Docklands.

## Planning a Journey

The London Travel Information Call Centre, Tel: (020) 7222 1234 (MINICOM (020) 7918 3015) will answer queries about timetables and fares and give journey planning advice for all public transport services in the London area. The Information Call Centre operates 24 hours a day and has an automatic queuing system for telephone callers. There are London Travel Information Centres at the following Underground stations; Euston, Heathrow, Liverpool Street, King's Cross St. Pancras, Oxford Circus, Piccadilly Circus, St. James's Park and Victoria. For the latest travel updates, call Travel Check Tel: (020) 7222 1200 (open 24 hours). You can also access information from London Transport's website: www.londontransport.co.uk.

---

\* One day travelcards valid after 9.30am Mon-Fri or anytime Sat and Sun.
° You must have a valid ticket for your entire journey or you may be liable to penalty fines.

# **4** How To Use This Guide

This guide is specifically designed to get you to any place in Central London from the nearest or most appropriate Underground station. It is intended for travellers who wish to use the Underground to take them to the nearest Underground station and then walk to their destination. Therefore, all the places shown in the guide are within easy walking distance of the Underground station.

For the purposes of this guide the nearest station has been arrived at by taking a straight-line distance from the Underground station in the centre of the map, to the centre point of the square in which the given street or place of interest falls. It is, therefore, just an approximation and may not always be the nearest station when following the streets on foot. The average straight-line distance from the station to the street or place of interest is about 300 metres on the 1:10,000 scale maps and 600 metres on the 1:20,000 scale maps.

**NB.** Not every Underground station is contained within this guide. The Underground stations shown have been included because of their location and strategic importance. The **Index to Streets** lists only those streets which are named on the maps.

## How to Find a Street or Place of Interest

Look in either the **Index to Street Names** or the **Index to Places of Interest** to find the street or place of interest you wish to visit. Alongside the name in the index you will find the nearest or most appropriate Underground station to your destination, along with the page number and grid reference.

**Example:**

| Abbots La. | SE1 | London Br. | 45 | D3 |
|:---:|:---:|:---:|:---:|:---:|
| Street Name | Postal District | Nearest Tube Station | Page No. | Grid Reference |

In this example you will find Abbots Lane on page 45 in square D3. Its nearest tube station is London Bridge which is in the centre of the map on that page.

The same sequence is followed for the **Index to Places of Interest** except that the street name becomes the place of interest and postal districts are not always given.

In some cases different Underground stations appear on the same indexed street or road. In these cases the Underground stations are indexed to the nearest point along the street or road on which they fall. This can be North (N), Central (Cen), South (S), West (W) or East (E).

**Example:**

| | | | |
|---|---|---|---|
| Borough High St. (N) SE1 | London Br. | 45 | A4 |
| Borough High St. (Cen) SE1 | Boro. | 17 | B3 |

In this example, if your destination is at the north end of Borough High Street, found in square A4, your nearest Underground station would be London Bridge on page 45. If your destination is at the centre of Borough High Street, found in square B3, your nearest Underground station would be Borough on page 17.

Some streets and places of interest are referenced to Underground stations which are not shown separately, but fall within the area of another mapped Underground station.

**Example:**

| | | | |
|---|---|---|---|
| Albany St. NW1 | Morn Cres. | 18 | B4 |

Albany Street, in postal district NW1, is listed as being nearest to Mornington Crescent Station and can be found within the Camden Town area map on page 18 in square B4. There is no separate map for Mornington Crescent Underground station.

Some streets and places of interest may, in reality, be closer to an Underground station which has not been included in this guide. In these cases they are referenced to the nearest mapped Underground station. Some streets and places of interest which do not fall within 'easy walking distance' of the Central London Underground stations shown may not appear in this guide.

# Exits

In order to get your bearings when reaching the Underground station, the exit streets are listed beneath the map. Please note that a small number of exits shown may be subject to restricted opening hours.

Information for disabled travellers may be provided by the unit for Disabled Passengers - tel and minicom (020) 7918 3312.

# Places of Interest

As well as being separately indexed, main places of interest are listed and referenced on the same page as their nearest Underground station.
(Not all map pages have important places of interest within their area).

# 6 Underground stations

# Key to Map Symbols

This key refers to symbols used on pages 10-73, except pages 18-19, 24, 35-36, 51-52 & 72.

| | | | |
|---|---|---|---|
| **A40(M)** | Motorway | ■ POL ■ Fire Sta | Police/Fire station |
| Dual **A4** | Primary route | ■ PO ■ Lib | Post office/Library |
| Dual **A40** | 'A' road | ℹ | Tourist information centre |
| **B504** | 'B' road | P WC | Car park/Public toilet |
| | Other road | 📽 ▣ | Cinema/Theatre |
| → | One way street | ⊠ ■ USA | Major hotel/Embassy |
| | Street market | + ■ Mormon | Church/Other place of worship |
| | Pedestrian street | ☾ ✡ | Mosque/Synagogue |
| ▪ ▬ | Access restriction | | Leisure & tourism |
| ------- ------ | Track/Footpath | | Shopping |
| — — — | Pedestrian ferry | | Administration & law |
| CITY | Borough boundary | | Health & welfare |
| EC2 | Postal district boundary | | Education |
| ⇤ ⇥ | Main/Other railway station | | Industry & commerce |
| ⊖ | Tube station* | | Public open space |
| ⊸ | DLR station | | Park/Garden/Sports ground |
| ● | Bus/Coach station | ↑↑↑ | Cemetery |

**Scale 1:10,000 (6.3 inches to 1 mile)**

| 0 | ¼ | ½ km |
|---|---|---|
| 0 | | ¼ mile |

\* The featured tube station per page is shown as an enlarged symbol

# Key to Map Symbols

This key refers to symbols used on pages 18-19, 24, 35-36, 51-52 & 72

| | | | |
|---|---|---|---|
| **M4** | Motorway | Pol Fire Sta | Police/Fire station |
| Dual **A4** | Primary route | PO Lib | Post office/Library |
| Dual **A40** | 'A' road | i | Tourist information centre |
| **B504** | 'B' road | P WC | Car park/Public toilet |
| | Other road | USA | Embassy |
| → | One way street/Toll | + Mormon | Church/Other place of worship |
| | Street market | ☾ ✡ | Mosque/Synagogue |
| | Pedestrian street | | Leisure & tourism |
| | Access restriction | | Shopping |
| ----- | Track/Cycle path/Footpath | | Administration & law |
| | County boundary | | Health & welfare |
| | Borough boundary | | Education |
| | Postal district boundary | | Industry & commerce |
| ⇥ ⇥ | Main/other railway station | | Public open space |
| ⬯ | Tube station* | | Park/Garden/Sports ground |
| ⬤ | DLR station | | Golf course |
| ⬤ | Bus/Coach station | | Woodland |
| | | | Cemetery |

## Scale 1:20,000 (3.2 inches to 1 mile)

| 0 | ½ | 1 km |
|---|---|---|
| 0 | | ½ mile |

* The featured tube station per page is shown as an enlarged symbol

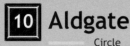

# 10 Aldgate | Aldgate East

- Circle
- Metropolitan

- District
- Hammersmith & City

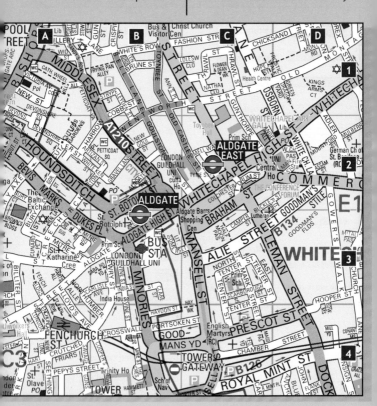

**Exits:** ALDGATE - Aldgate High St
ALDGATE EAST - West End - Whitechapel High St(N&S); Leman St(W&E);
Braham St(N&S). East End - Whitechapel High St(N&S); Commercial Rd(N)

**Places of Interest:** Conference Forum, The C2; Toynbee Hall C2;
Whitechapel Art Gallery C2

# Baker Street

| | |
|---|---|
| ■■■ Bakerloo | ■■■ Jubilee |
| ■■■ Circle | ■■■ Metropolitan |
| ■■■ Hammersmith & City | |

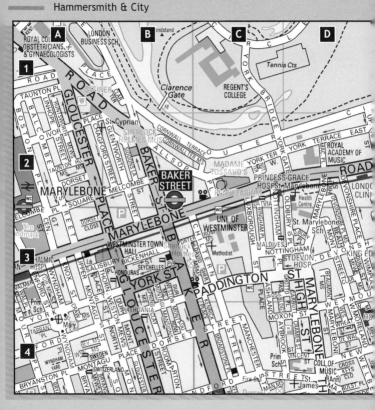

**Exits:** Metropolitan - Marylebone Rd (N&S)
Bakerloo/Jubilee - Marylebone Rd (N); Baker St

**Places of Interest:** Baker Street B2; Madame Tussaud's C2;
Planetarium C2; Sherlock Holmes Museum B2

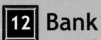

# 12 Bank

| | |
|---|---|
| ▬▬▬ Central | ▬▬▬ Northern |
| ▬▬▬ Docklands Light Railway | ▬▬▬ Waterloo & City |

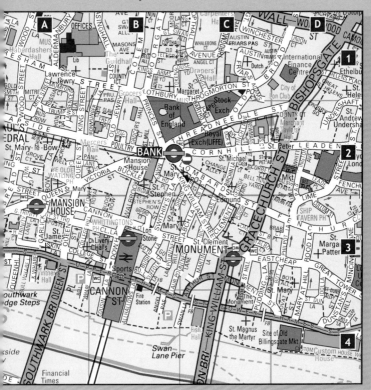

**Exits:** Princes St(W&E); Threadneedle St(N&S); Cornhill(N&S); Lombard St(N&S); Mansion House Place; Queen Victoria St(N&S); (Subway Link to MONUMENT)

**Places of Interest:** Bank of England B2; Bank of England Museum C2; Guildhall, The B1; Mansion House B2; Royal Exchange (L.I.F.F.E.) C2; Stock Exchange C2

# Barbican

Circle
Hammersmith & City
Metropolitan

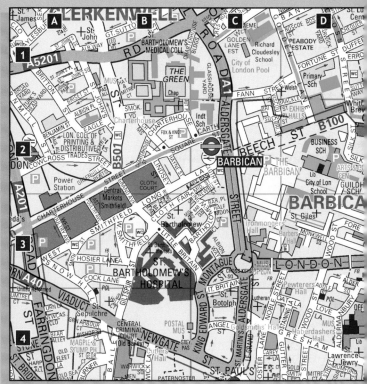

**Exits:** Aldersgate St

**Places of Interest:** Barbican Arts and Conference Centre D2; Charterhouse B2; Museum of London C3; St. Bartholomew-the-Great Church, Cloth Fair EC1 B3; Smithfield Central Market B3

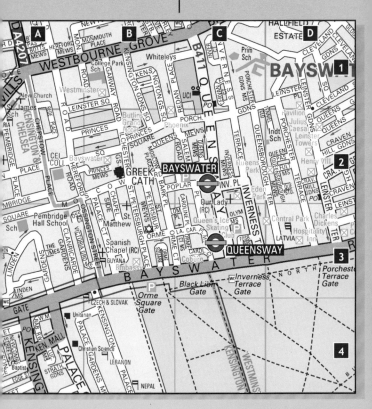

**Exits:** BAYSWATER - Queensway
QUEENSWAY - Queensway/Bayswater Rd

**Places of Interest:** Queen's Ice Rink C3

# Blackfriars

— Circle
— District

**Exits:** BR Station; Queen Victoria St(N&S); Blackfriars Bridge (W&E); Riverside Walkway; Victoria Embankment(N); New Bridge St(W)

**Places of Interest:** Bankside Gallery C4; College of Arms C3; Doctor Johnson's House, Gough Sq. EC4 A2; Fleet Street A2; H.M.S. 'President' A3; St. Bride's Church and Crypt Museum B2; St. Bride's Printing Library, Bride La. EC4 B2; Y.H.A., Carter La. EC4 C2

# 16 Bond Street

━━━ Central
━━━ Jubilee

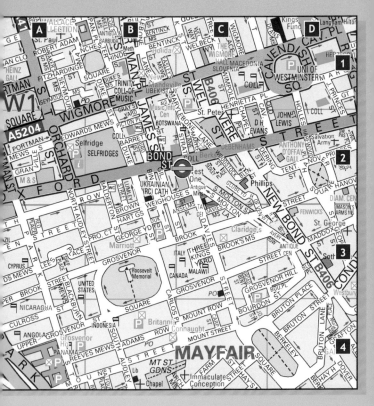

**Exits:** Oxford St (N&S); West One Shopping Centre; Gilbert St; Davies St

**Places of Interest:** Selfridges B2

# Borough

━━━ Northern

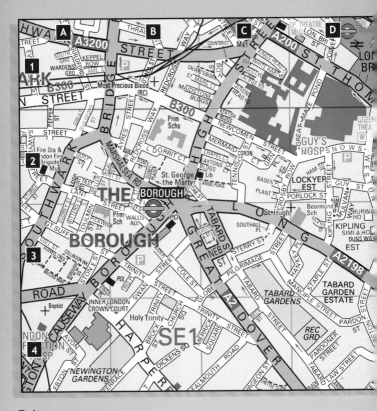

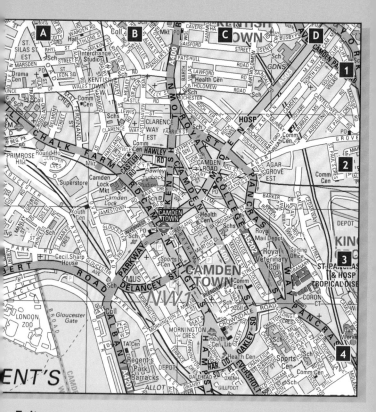

**Exits:** Kentish Town Road; Camden High Street

**Places of Interest:** Camden Lock Market and Waterbuses B2; Cecil Sharp House A3; Jewish Museum B3; London Zoo A4; London Wildlife Trust, Camley St. NW1 D3

# Canary Wharf

━━━ Docklands Light Railway
━━━ Jubilee

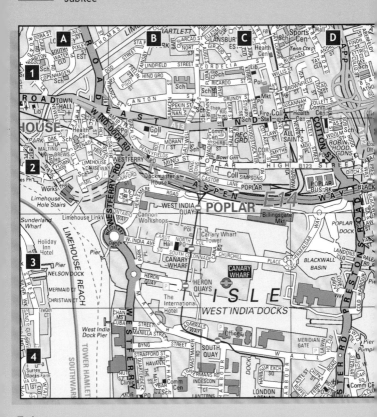

**Exits:** North Colonnade; South Colonnade; Cabot Place(E&W)

**Places of Interest:** Billingsgate Fish Market C3; Canary Wharf Tower, Isle of Dogs C3; Docklands Visitors Centre D4; London Arena C4; Surrey Docks Farm A4

# 20 Cannon Street

Circle
District

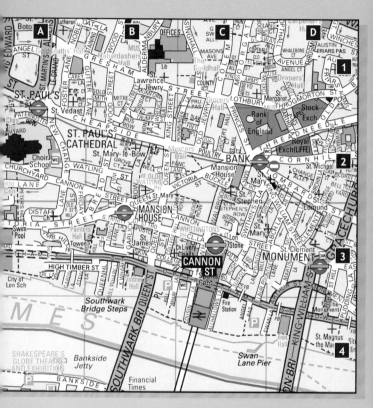

**Exits:** BR Station; Cannon St; Dowgate Hill

**Places of Interest:** London Stone C3; Skinners' Hall, Dowgate Hill EC4 C3

# Chancery Lane

Central (closed Sundays)

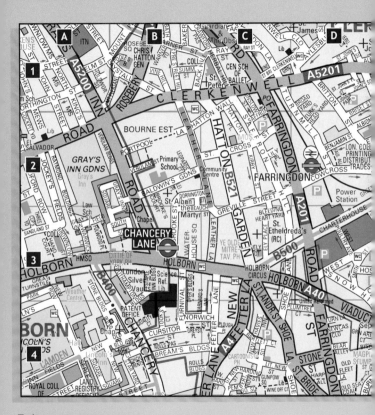

**Exits:** Holborn(N&S); Grays Inn Rd(W&E)

**Places of Interest:** Gray's Inn  A2; London Silver Vaults  B3; Patent Office  B4; Science Reference Library  B3

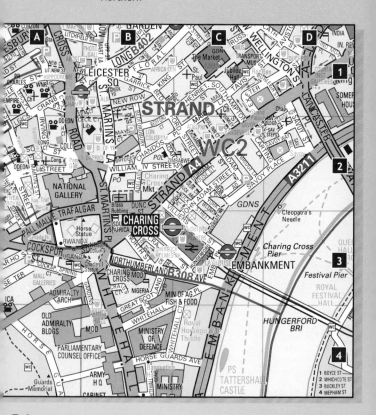

**Exits:** Main Booking Hall - BR Station; Strand(N&S); William IV St; The Courtyard; Villiers St. Trafalgar Sq Booking Hall - Trafalgar Sq; The Mall; Strand (N); Duncannon St(W)

**Places of Interest:** Admiralty Arch A3; Banqueting House B4; Coliseum, The B2; Horse Guards Parade A4; Institute of Contemporary Arts A3; London Brass Rubbing Centre B2; Mall Galleries A3; Nelson's Column B3; St. Martin-in-the-Fields Church B2; Victoria Embankment Gardens C2

# Covent Garden

Piccadilly

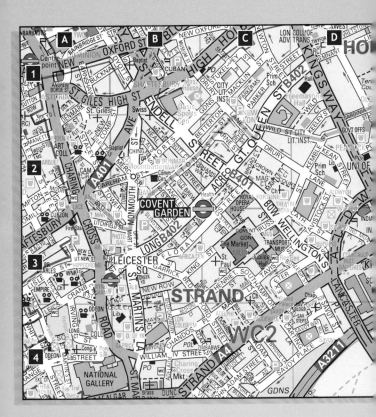

**Exits:** Long Acre

**Places of Interest:** Cabaret Mechanical Theatre, Covent Garden  C3;
Covent Garden  C3; London Transport Museum, Covent Gdn.  WC2  C3; Royal
Opera House  C2; Theatre Museum, Russell St.  WC2  C3; Theatre Royal, Drury
La.  WC2  C2

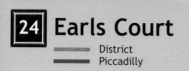

# 24 Earls Court

— District
— Piccadilly

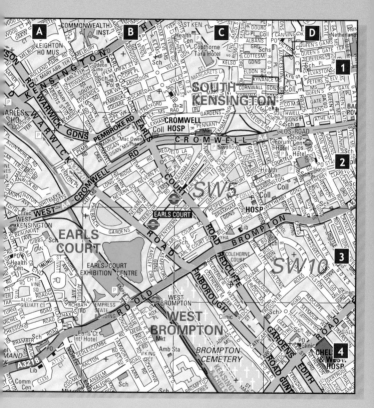

**Exits:** Exhibition Hall; Earl's Ct Rd; Warwick Rd

**Places of Interest:** Earls Court Exhibition Centre  B3; Y.H.A., Earl's Ct. SW5  C3

# Edgware Road

- Bakerloo
- Circle
- District
- Hammersmith & City

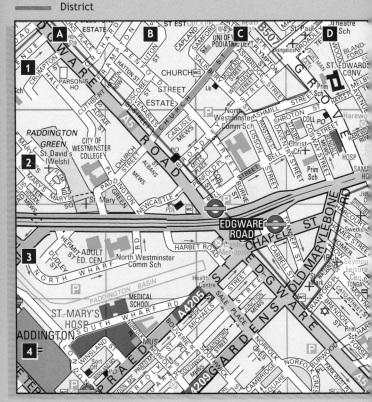

**Exits:** Bakerloo - Edgware Rd/Marylebone Rd.
Circle/District/Hammersmith and City - Chapel St; Marylebone Rd(S)

**Exits:** Bakerloo - Elephant and Castle(N).
Northern - BR Station; Elephant and Castle(S); Shopping Centre

**Places of Interest:** Cuming Museum C4

# Embankment

| | |
|---|---|
| ▬▬▬ Bakerloo | ▬▬▬ Northern |
| ▬▬▬ Circle | |
| ▬▬▬ District | |

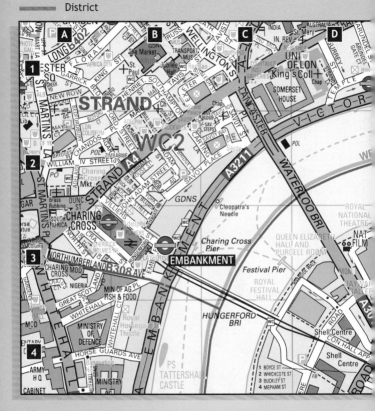

**Exits:** Victoria Embankment; Villiers St

**Places of Interest:** Cleopatra's Needle  C3; P.S. 'Tattershall Castle'  B4

# 28 Euston

—— Northern
—— Victoria

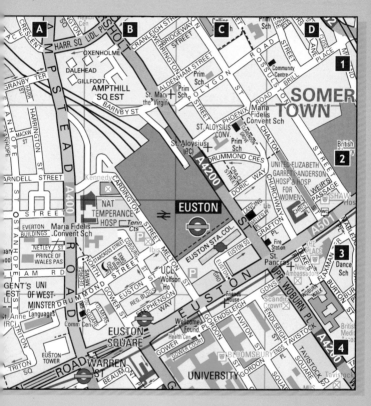

**Exits:** BR Station; Suburban Platforms 8-11

**Places of Interest:** British Library D2

# Euston Square

Circle
Hammersmith & City
Metropolitan

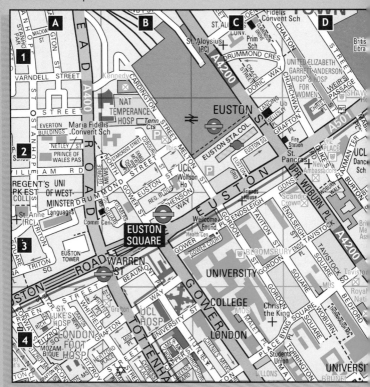

**Exits:** Euston Rd(N&S)

**Places of Interest:** University College London C3; Wellcome Trust, Euston Rd. NW1 C3

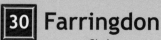

# 30 Farringdon

Circle
Hammersmith & City
Metropolitan

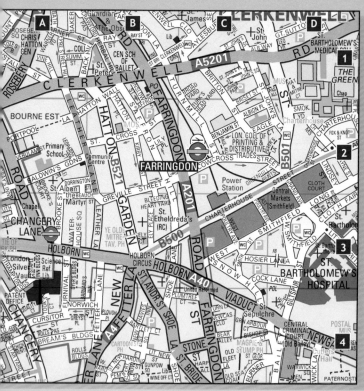

**Exits:** Cowcross St; Turnmill St

**Places of Interest:** National Museum of Cartoon Art B2; St. John's Gate and Museum of the Order of St. John C1

# Gloucester Road

— Circle
— District
— Piccadilly

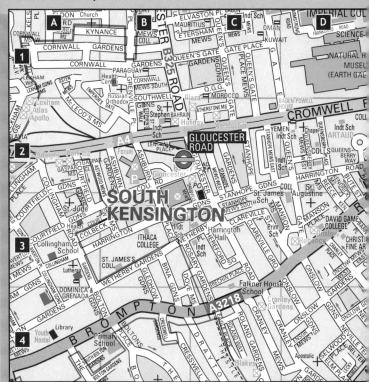

**Exits:** Gloucester Rd

**Places of Interest:** Baden-Powell House  C2

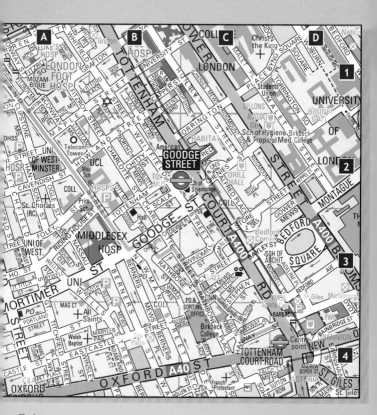

**Exits:** Tottenham Ct Rd

**Places of Interest:** Brunei Gallery, Thornhaugh St. WC1 D2; Petri Museum of Egyptian Archaeology, Malet Pl. WC1 C1; Pollock's Toy Museum B2; Royal Academy of Dramatic Art (R.A.D.A.) C2; Telecom Tower A2

# Great Portland Street

- Circle
- Hammersmith & City
- Metropolitan

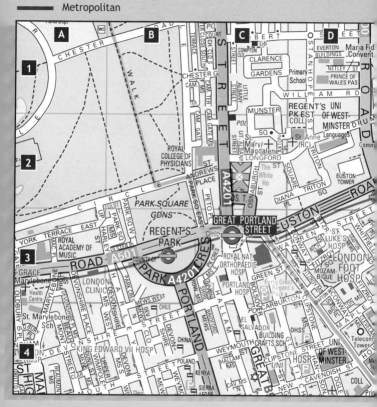

**Exits:** Gt Portland St(E); Marylebone Rd(S)

# 34 Green Park

 ▬▬▬ Jubilee
 ▬▬▬ Piccadilly
 ▬▬▬ Victoria

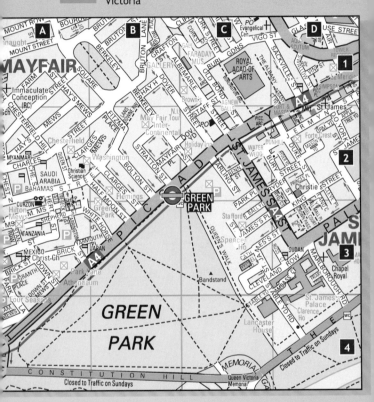

**Exits:** Green Park; Piccadilly(N&S); Stratton St

**Places of Interest:** Agnew Galleries C1; Burlington Arcade, Burlington Gdns. W1 C1; Faraday Museum C1; Green Park B4; Lancaster House C4; Marlborough House D3; Medici Galleries, Grafton St. W1 B1; Pall Mall D3; Royal Academy of Arts C1; Spencer House, St. James's Pl. SW1 C3

# Hammersmith

- District
- Hammersmith & City
- Piccadilly

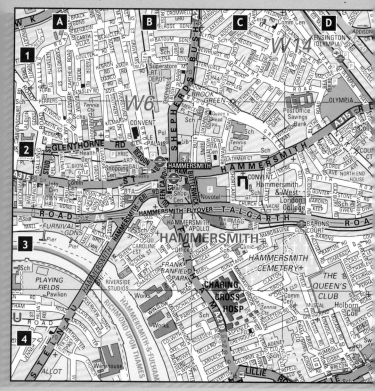

**Exits:** District/Piccadilly - Hammersmith Broadway(S); Queen Charlotte St(W&E); Hammersmith Bridge(N&S); Bus Station
Hammersmith & City - Beadon Road; Hammersmith Broadway(N)

**Places of Interest:** Apollo Labatts (Hammersmith) B3; Le Palais, Hammersmith B2; Lyric Art Gallery, King St. W6 B2; Olympia D1; Queens Club (Tennis Centre) D3

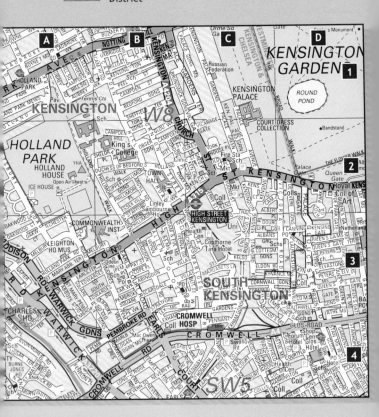

**Exits:** Kensington High St

**Places of Interest:** Commonwealth Institute  A3; Court Dress Collection,
Kensington Palace  C2; Kensington Gardens  D1; Leighton House Museum,
Holland Park Rd.  W14  A3; Linley Sambourne House, Stafford Ter.  W8  B2;
Royal College of Art  D2

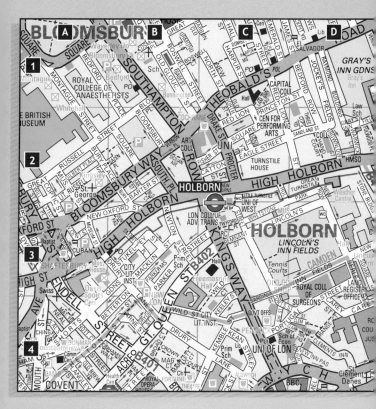

**Exits:** High Holborn

**Places of Interest:** Bloomsbury Square B2; Freemason's Hall (United Grand Lodge of England) B3; Lincoln's Inn D3; Old Curiosity Shop C3; Royal College of Surgeons D3; Sir John Soane's Museum, Lincoln's Inn Fields WC2 C3

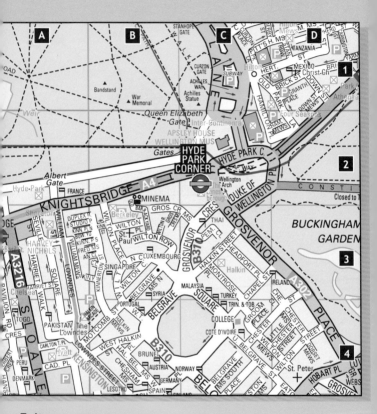

**Exits:** Hyde Pk Corner(N&S); Knightsbridge(N&S); Grosvenor Place (W)

**Places of Interest:** Apsley House, Wellington Museum C2; Hyde Park Corner C2; Wellington Arch C2

# King's Cross St. Pancras

**Legend:**
- Circle
- Hammersmith & City
- Metropolitan
- Northern
- Piccadilly
- Victoria

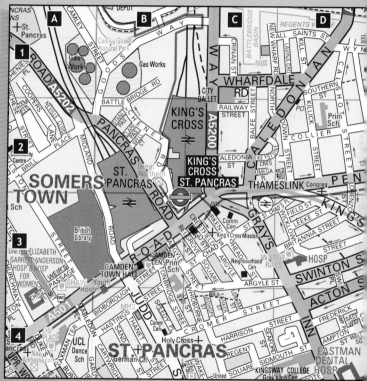

**Exits:** Kings Cross BR Station; St Pancras BR Station; Euston Rd (N&S); Pancras Rd(W); Pentonville Rd(S); BR Thameslink

**Places of Interest:** Camley Street Natural Park B1; London Canal Museum, The C1; Salvation Army International Heritage Centre, Judd St. WC1 B4

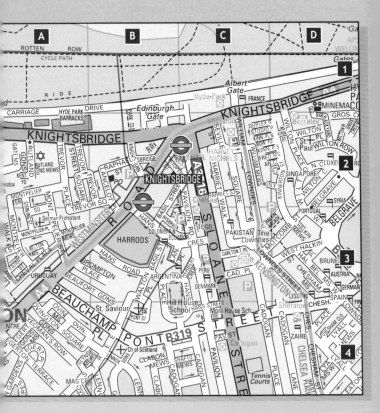

**Exits:** Knightsbridge(N&S); Brompton Rd (W&E); Sloane St

**Places of Interest:** Harrods B3

# Lambeth North

Bakerloo

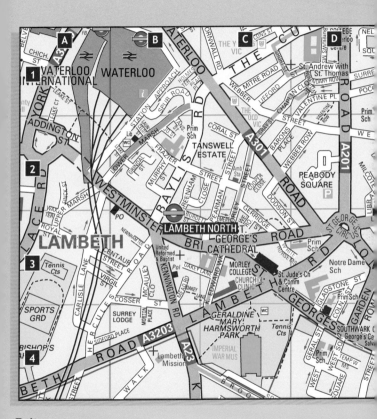

**Exits:** Westminster Bridge Rd

**Places of Interest:** Imperial War Museum C4

# 42 Lancaster Gate

Central

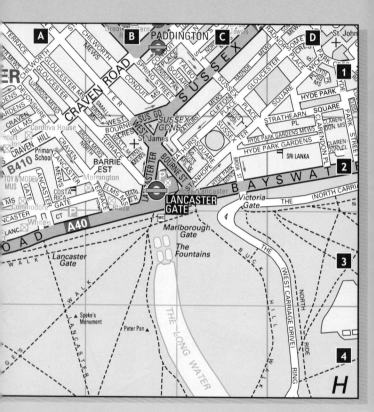

**Exits:** Bayswater Rd

**Places of Interest:** Hyde Park D4; London Toy and Model Museum, Craven Hill A2; Peter Pan Statue B4

# Leicester Square

— Northern
— Piccadilly

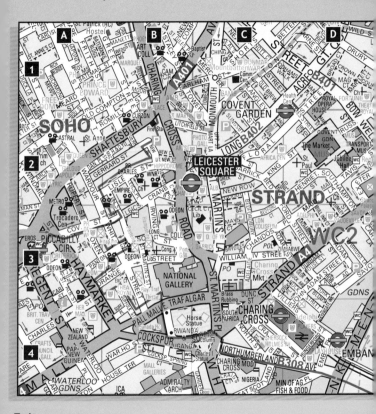

**Exits:** Charing Cross Rd(N&S); Cranbourne St

**Places of Interest:** Africa Centre, King St. WC2 C2; Leicester Square B3; National Gallery B3; National Portrait Gallery B3; Photographers' Gallery, Great Newport St. WC2 C2

# 44 Liverpool Street

Central
Circle
Hammersmith & City
Metropolitan

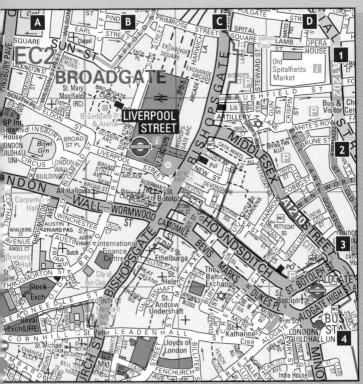

**Exits:** BR Station; Liverpool St(N&S); Old Broad St

**Places of Interest:** Broadgate Ice and Arena B2; International Finance Centre B3; Old Spitalfields Market and Opera House D1; Petticoat Lane (Market) C2

# London Bridge

━━━ Northern
━━━ Jubilee

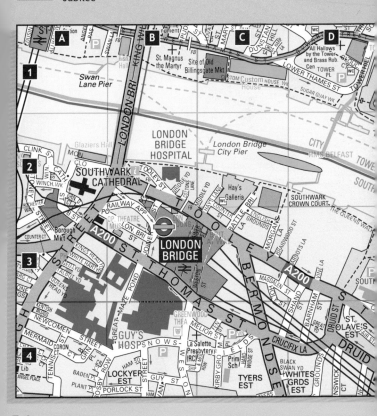

**Exits:** BR Station; Bus Station/Forecourt; Duke St Hill

**Places of Interest:** Borough Market A3; Britain at War Experience C3; George Inn, Borough High St. SE1 A3; Hay's Galleria C2; London Bridge B2; London Dungeon B3; Operating Theatre Museum and Herb Garret B3; Southwark Cathedral A2

Circle
District

**Exits:** Queen Victoria St(NSE&W); Bow Lane; Garlick Hill; Cannon St(NS&W)

**Places of Interest:** St. Mary-le-Bow Church C2; Shakespeare Globe Theatre and Exhibition B4; Temple of Mithras, Queen Victoria St. EC4 C2

# Marble Arch

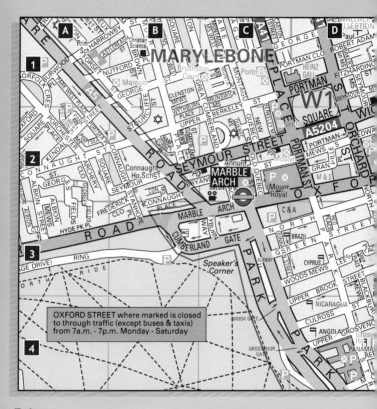

**Exits:** Marble Arch; Park Lane(W&E); Oxford St(N&S)

**Places of Interest:** Heinz Gallery, R.I.B.A. D1; Marble Arch C3; Speaker's Corner C3; Wallace Collection D1

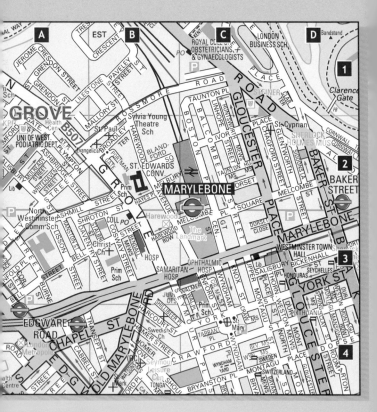

**Exits:** BR Station

# Monument

— Circle
— District

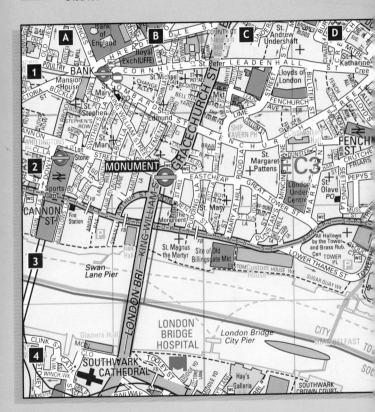

**Exits:** Cannon St; Fish St Hill; Great Tower St; King William St; (Subway Link to BANK)

**Places of Interest:** Custom House  C3; Leadenhall Market  C1; Lloyds of London  C1; Monument, The  B2; St. Mary at Hill Church, Lovat La.  EC3  C2

# 50 Moorgate

Circle
Hamersmith & City
Metropolitan
Northern

**Exits:** Moorgate(W&E); Moorfields(W&E); BR Thameslink

# North Greenwich for the Dome

Jubilee

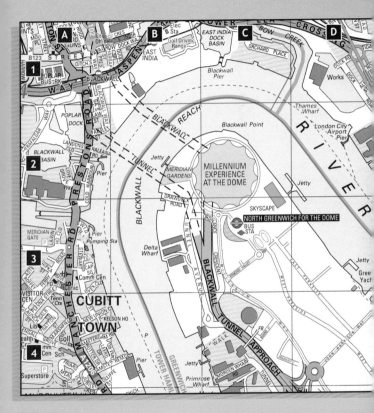

**Exits:** Bus Station / Millenium Dome

**Places of Interest:** Millennium Experience at the Dome C2

Central
Circle
District

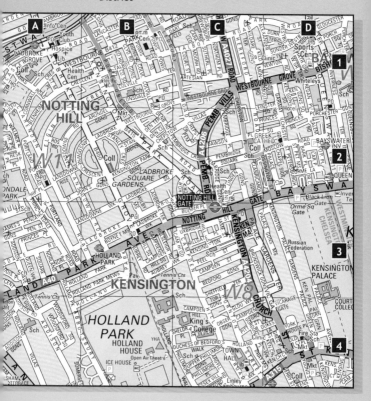

**Exits:** Notting Hill Gate(N&S)

**Places of Interest:** Holland House and Park B4; Kensington Palace D3; Y.H.A., Holland Ho. W8 B4

# Old Street

— Northern

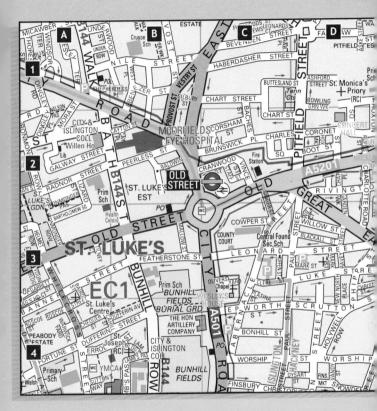

**Exits:** Old St(NS&W); City Rd(NS&W)

**Places of Interest:** Wesley's House C3; Whitbread Shire Horse Stables, Garrett St. EC1 A3

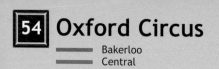

# 54 Oxford Circus

Bakerloo
Central
Victoria

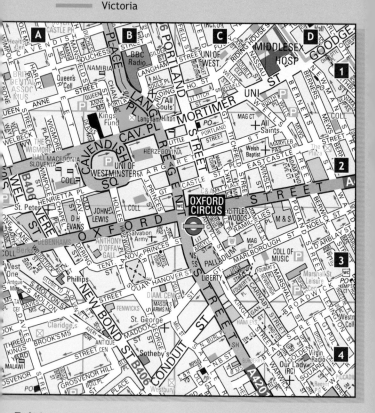

**Exits:** Oxford St(NSE&W); Regent St(NSE&W); Argyll St

**Places of Interest:** Anthony d'Offay Gallery B3; B.B.C. Experience, Portland Pl. W1 B1; Carnaby Street C3; Hamleys C4; Liberty C3; London Palladium C3; Oxford Circus C3; Oxford Street B3; Regent Street B2; Sotheby's B4

# Paddington

Bakerloo

Circle

District

Hammersmith & City

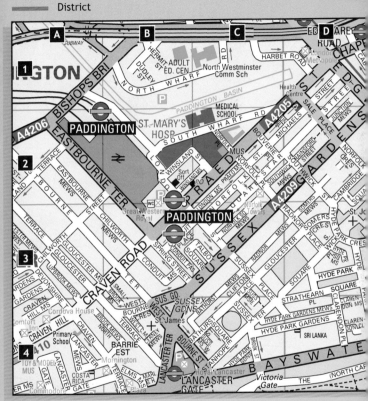

**Exits:** BR Station; Praed St

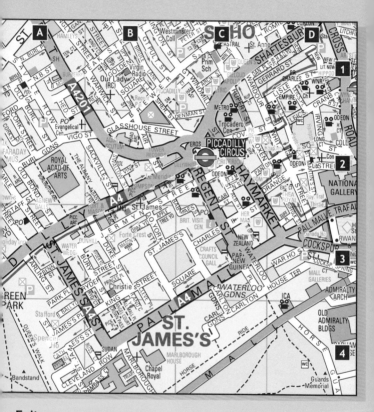

**Exits:** Piccadilly(N&S); Regent St(NSE&W); Coventry St; London Pavilion; Centre at the Circus

**Places of Interest:** Chinatown, Gerrard St. W1 C1; Christie's B3; Crafts Council Gallery, Waterloo Pl. SW1 C3; Eros C2; Fortnum and Mason B3; Piccadilly Circus C2; Rock Circus, London Pavilion C2; Soho C1; Trocadero Centre C2

# Pimlico

Victoria

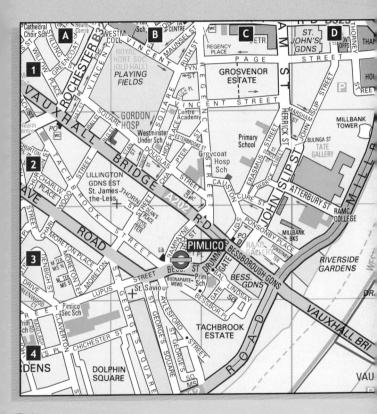

**Exits:** Bessborough St(N&S); Rampayne St

**Places of Interest:** R.A.A.B. Gallery C3; Royal Horticultural Society (Old Hall) B1; Tate Gallery D2; Thames House D1

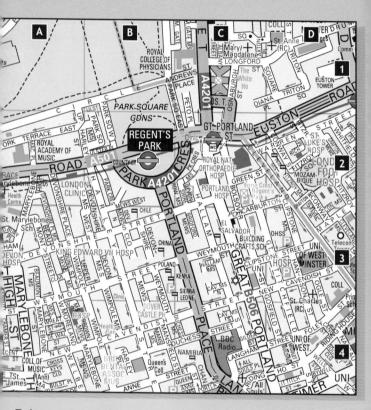

**Exits:** Marylebone Rd

**Places of Interest:** British Dental Association Museum, Wimpole St.  B4;
Royal Academy of Music  A2

# Russell Square

—— Piccadilly

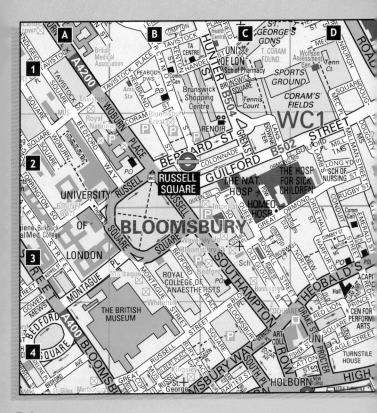

**Exits:** Bernard St

**Places of Interest:** British Medical Association  A1; Dickens House, Doughty St.  WC1  D2; Percival David Foundation of Chinese Art, Gordon Sq. WC1  A2; University of London  A2

# 60 St. James's Park

Circle
District

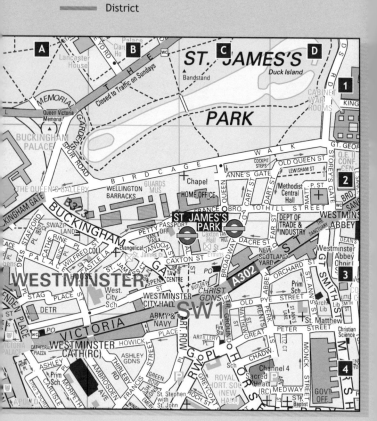

**Exits:** Broadway; Palmer St; Petty France

**Places of Interest:** Buckingham Palace A2; Caxton Hall C3; City of Westminster Archives Centre, The D3; Clarence House B1; Guards Museum B2; Home Office C2; New Scotland Yard C3; Queen Victoria Memorial A1; Queen's Gallery, The A2; Royal Horticultural Society (New Hall) C4; St. James's Palace B1; Westminster Abbey D2; Westminster City Hall B3

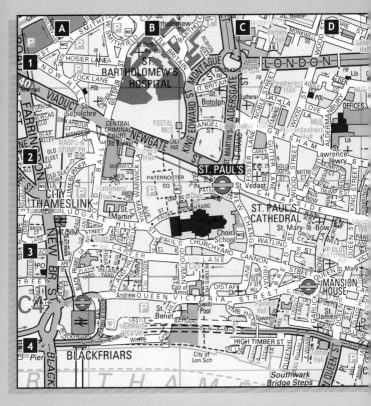

**Exits:** St Martin's Le Grand/Cheapside; Newgate St

**Places of Interest:** Central Criminal Court (Old Bailey) B2; Chartered Insurance Institutes Museum, Aldermanbury EC2 D2; Clockmakers Company Collection, The, Guildhall Library D2; Goldsmiths' Hall C2; Guildhall Art Gallery, Guildhall Library D2; National Postal Museum B2; St. Lawrence Jewry Church, Gresham St. EC2 D2; St. Paul's Cathedral C3

# 62 Sloane Square

Circle
District

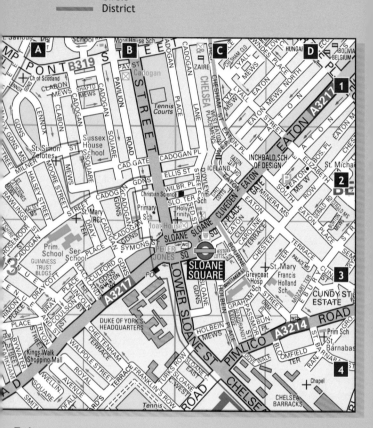

**Exits:** Sloane Square

# South Kensington

Circle
District
Piccadilly

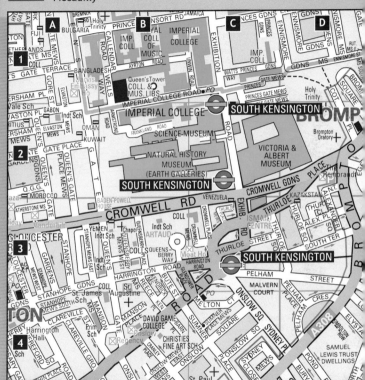

**Exits:** Exhibition Rd(W&E); Cromwell Rd; Natural History Museum; Pelham St; Thurloe St

**Places of Interest:** Brompton Oratory D2; Earth Galleries B2; Imperial College B1; Ismaili Centre and Zamana Gallery C3; Museum of Instruments, B1; Natural History Museum B2; Queen's Tower B1; Royal College of Music B1; Science Museum B2; Victoria and Albert Museum C2

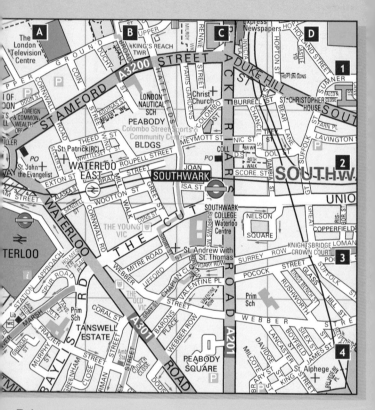

**Exits:** Blackfriars Rd/The Cut; (Subway Link to BR Waterloo East)

# Temple

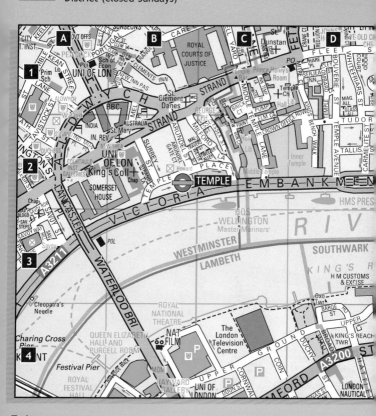

Circle (closed Sundays)
District (closed Sundays)

**Exits:** Temple Place/Victoria Embankment

**Places of Interest:** Courtauld Institute Galleries  A2; H.Q.S. Wellington, Master Mariners' Hall  C3; Prince Henry's Room  C1; Public Record Office Museum  C1; Roman Bath  WC2  B2; Royal Courts of Justice  B1; St. Clement Danes Church  B1; Somerset House  A2; Temple Bar  C1; Temple, The  C2

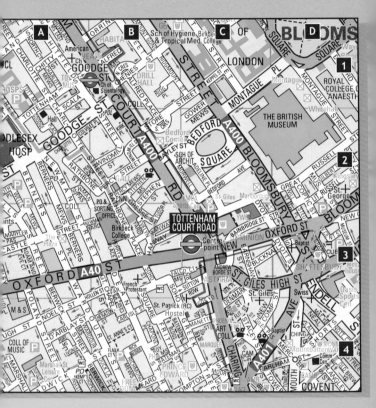

**Exits:** Tottenham Ct Rd(W&E); Oxford St(N&S); New Oxford St(N&S); Charing Cross Rd(E); Centre Point

**Places of Interest:** British Museum C2; Centrepoint C3; Dominion Theatre C3; Y.M.C.A. C2; Y.W.C.A. C3

Circle
District

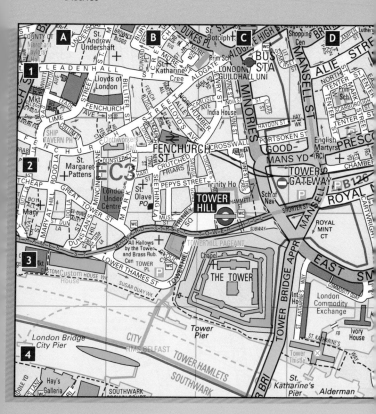

**Exits:** Trinity Square

**Places of Interest:** H.M.S. 'Belfast' B4; London Commodity Exchange D3; Tower Hill C3; Tower Pier B4; Tower of London C3; Trinity House C2

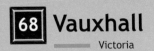

# 68 Vauxhall

Victoria

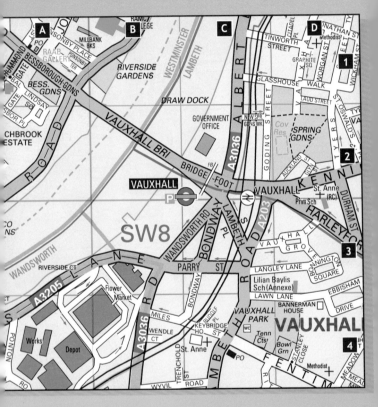

**Exits:** BR Station; Kennington Lane; Bondway(W&E); Wandsworth Rd; Albert Embankment(River Side)

**Places of Interest:** Flower Market, New Covent Garden Market  B3

# Victoria

Circle
District
Victoria

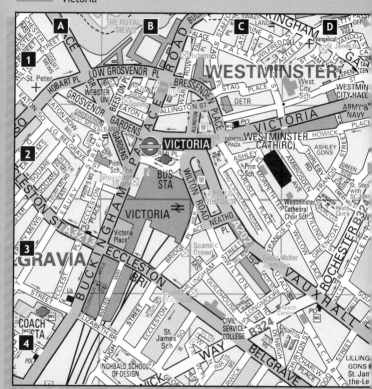

**Exits:** Victoria Line Booking Hall - BR Station; Wilton Rd.
District/Circle Booking Hall - Victoria St; Terminus Place; (Subway link to Victoria line booking hall)

**Places of Interest:** Apollo Victoria Theatre C2; Department of the Environment, Transport and Regions C1; Royal Mews, The B1; Victoria Coach Station A4; Westminster Cathedral C2

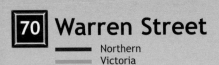

# 70 Warren Street

— Northern
— Victoria

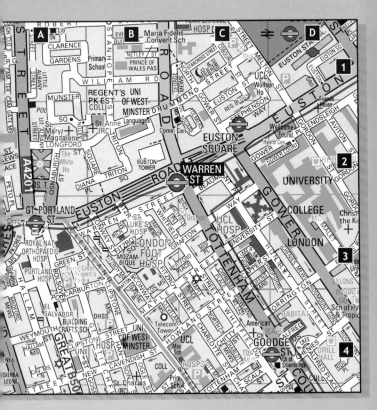

**Exits:** Warren St; Tottenham Ct Rd(W)

# Waterloo

Bakerloo            Waterloo & City
Jubilee
Northern

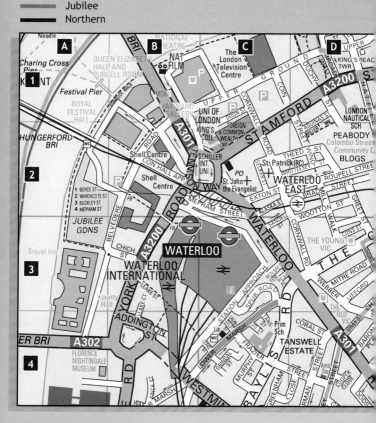

**Exits:** BR Station; York Rd(N&S); Waterloo Rd

**Places of Interest:** County Hall A3; Florence Nightingale Museum A4; Hayward Gallery B1; Jubilee Gardens A3; London Aquarium, County Hall A3; Museum of the Moving Image (M.O.M.I.) B1; Queen Elizabeth Hall and Purcell Room A1; Royal Festival Hall A1; Royal National Theatre B1; Shell Centre B2

Jubilee
Metropolitan

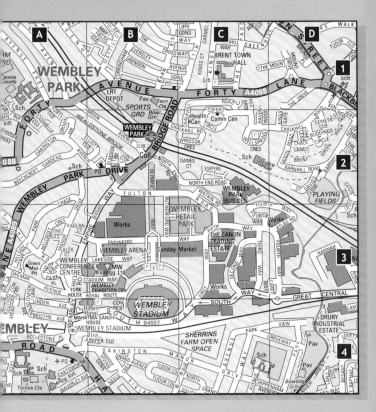

**Exits:** Bridge Rd; (Subway Link to Stadium Way)

**Places of Interest:** Wembley Conference Centre  A3; Wembley Stadium
B4

# Westminster

Circle
District
Jubilee

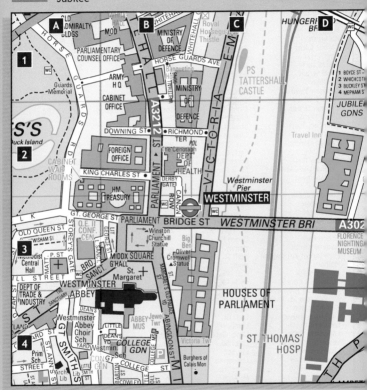

**Exits:** Westminster Bridge; Victoria Embankment(W&E); Parliament St(E); Bridge St(N); Westminster Pier

**Places of Interest:** Big Ben B3; Cabinet War Rooms A2; Cenotaph, The B2; Downing Street B2; Houses of Parliament C4; Jewel Tower, Houses of Parliament B4; Middlesex Guildhall B3; Victoria Tower, Houses of Parliament B4; Westminster Abbey Museum B4; Westminster Pier C2

## Tube Station Abbreviations

| | |
|---|---|
| Aldgate | Ald. |
| Aldgate East | Ald. E. |
| Baker Street | Baker St. |
| Bank | Bank |
| Barbican | Barb. |
| Barons Court | Bar. Ct. |
| Bayswater | Bays. |
| Blackfriars | Black. |
| Bond Street | Bond St. |
| Borough | Boro. |
| Camden Town | Cam. Tn. |
| Canary Wharf | Can. Wf. |
| Cannon Street | Cann. St. |
| Chalk Farm | Chalk Fm. |
| Chancery Lane | Chan. La. |
| Charing Cross | Char. X |
| Covent Garden | Cov. Gdn. |
| Earls Court | Earls Ct. |
| Edgware Road | Edgw. Rd. |
| Elephant & Castle | El. & Cas. |
| Embankment | Embk. |
| Euston | Euston |
| Euston Square | Euston Sq. |
| Farringdon | Farr. |
| Gloucester Road | Glos. Rd. |
| Goodge Street | Goodge St. |
| Great Portland Street | Gt. Port. St. |
| Green Park | Green Pk. |
| Hammersmith | Hamm. |
| High Street Kensington | High St. Kens. |
| Holborn | Holb. |
| Holland Park | Holl. Pk. |
| Hyde Park Corner | Hyde Pk. Cor. |
| Kensington (Olympia) | Olym. |
| King's Cross St. Pancras | King's X |
| Knightsbridge | Knights. |
| Ladbroke Grove | Lad. Gr. |
| Lambeth North | Lamb. N. |
| Lancaster Gate | Lanc. Gate |
| Leicester Square | Leic. Sq. |
| Liverpool Street | Liv. St. |
| London Bridge | London Br. |
| Mansion House | Mans. Ho. |
| Marble Arch | M. Arch |
| Marylebone | Mary. |
| Monument | Mon. |
| Moorgate | Moor. |
| Mornington Crescent | Morn. Cres. |
| North Greenwich for the Dome | N. Green. |
| Notting Hill Gate | Nott. Hill Gate |
| Old Street | Old St. |
| Oxford Circus | Ox. Circ. |
| Paddington | Padd. |
| Piccadilly Circus | Picc. Circ. |
| Pimlico | Pim. |
| Queensway | Queens. |
| Ravenscourt Park | Ravens. Pk. |
| Regent's Park | Reg. Pk. |
| Russell Square | Russ. Sq. |
| St. James's Park | St. Jam. Pk. |
| St. Paul's | St. Paul's |
| Sloane Square | Sloane Sq. |
| South Kensington | S. Kens. |
| Southwark | S'wark |
| Temple | Temple |
| Tottenham Court Road | Tott. Ct. Rd. |
| Tower Hill | T. Hill |
| Vauxhall | Vaux. |
| Victoria | Vic. |
| Warren Street | Warr. St. |
| Waterloo | Water. |
| Wembley Park | Wem Pk. |
| West Brompton | W. Brom. |
| West Kensington | W. Kens. |
| Westminster | Westmin. |

## Other Abbreviations

| | |
|---|---|
| All. | Alley |
| Allot. | Allotments |
| Amb. | Ambulance |
| App. | Approach |
| Arc. | Arcade |
| Ave. | Avenue |
| Bdy. | Broadway |
| Bk. | Bank |
| Bldgs. | Buildings |
| Boul. | Boulevard |
| Bowl. | Bowling |
| Bri. | Bridge |
| C. of E. | Church of England |
| Cath. | Cathedral |
| Cem. | Cemetery |
| Cen. | Central, Centre |
| Cft. | Croft |
| Cfts. | Crofts |
| Ch. | Church |
| Chyd. | Churchyard |
| Cin. | Cinema |
| Circ. | Circus |
| Clo. | Close |
| Co. | County |
| Coll. | College |
| Comm. | Community |
| Conv. | Convent |
| Cor. | Corner |

| | | | |
|---|---|---|---|
| Coron. | Coroners | Ms. | Mews |
| Cors. | Corners | Mt. | Mount |
| Cotts. | Cottages | Mus. | Museum |
| Cov. | Covered | N. | North |
| Crem. | Crematorium | N.T. | National Trust |
| Cres. | Crescent | Nat. | National |
| Ct. | Court | P.H. | Public House |
| Cts. | Courts | P.O. | Post Office |
| Ctyd. | Courtyard | Par. | Parade |
| Dep. | Depot | Pas. | Passage |
| Dev. | Development | Pav. | Pavilion |
| Dr. | Drive | Pk. | Park |
| Dws. | Dwellings | Pl. | Place |
| E. | East | Pol. | Police |
| Ed. | Education | Prec. | Precinct |
| Elec. | Electricity | Prim. | Primary |
| Embk. | Embankment | Prom. | Promenade |
| Est. | Estate | Pt. | Point |
| Ex. | Exchange | Quad. | Quadrant |
| Exhib. | Exhibition | R.C. | Roman Catholic |
| F.B. | Footbridge | Rd. | Road |
| F.C. | Football Club | Rds. | Roads |
| Fld. | Field | Rec. | Recreation |
| Flds. | Fields | Res. | Reservoir |
| Fm. | Farm | Ri. | Rise |
| Gall. | Gallery | S. | South |
| Gar. | Garage | Sch. | School |
| Gdn. | Garden | Sec. | Secondary |
| Gdns. | Gardens | Shop. | Shopping |
| Govt. | Government | Sq. | Square |
| Gra. | Grange | St. | Saint |
| Grd. | Ground | St. | Street |
| Grds. | Grounds | Sta. | Station |
| Grn. | Green | Sts. | Streets |
| Grns. | Greens | Sub. | Subway |
| Gro. | Grove | Swim. | Swimming |
| Gros. | Groves | T.A. | Territorial Army |
| Ho. | House | T.H. | Town Hall |
| Hos. | Houses | Tenn. | Tennis |
| Hosp. | Hospital | Ter. | Terrace |
| Hts. | Heights | Thea. | Theatre |
| Ind. | Industrial | Trd. | Trading |
| Int. | International | Twr. | Tower |
| Junct. | Junction | Twrs. | Towers |
| La. | Lane | Uni. | University |
| Las. | Lanes | Vil. | Villa, Villas |
| Lib. | Library | Vw. | View |
| Lo. | Lodge | W. | West |
| Lwr. | Lower | Wd. | Wood |
| Mag. | Magistrates | Wds. | Woods |
| Mans. | Mansions | Wf. | Wharf |
| Mem. | Memorial | Wk. | Walk |
| Mkt. | Market | Wks. | Works |
| Mkts. | Markets | Yd. | Yard |

# Index to Street Names

| | | | |
|---|---|---|---|
| Allsop Pl. NW1 | Baker St. | 11 | B2 |
| Alma St. NW5 | Chalk Fm. | 18 | B1 |
| Alpha Gro. E14 | Can. Wf. | 19 | B4 |
| Ambassador's Ct. SW1 | Green Pk. | 34 | D3 |
| Ambrosden Ave. SW1 | St. Jam. Pk. | 60 | B4 |
| Amen Cor. EC4 | Black. | 15 | C2 |
| Amen Ct. EC4 | St. Paul's | 61 | B2 |
| America Sq. EC3 | T. Hill | 67 | C2 |
| America St. SE1 | Boro. | 17 | A1 |
| Amor Rd. W6 | Hamm. | 35 | B1 |
| Amoy Pl. E14 | Can. Wf. | 19 | B1 |
| Ampthill Sq. Est. NW1 | Euston | 28 | B1 |
| Ampton Pl. WC1 | King's X | 39 | D4 |
| Ampton St. WC1 | King's X | 39 | D4 |
| Amsterdam Rd. E14 | N. Green. | 51 | A4 |
| Anchor Yd. EC1 | Old St. | 53 | A3 |
| Ancill Clo. W6 | Bar. Ct. | 35 | D4 |
| Anderson St. SW3 | Sloane Sq. | 62 | A4 |
| Andrew Borde St. WC2 | Tott. Ct. Rd. | 66 | C3 |
| Andrew St. E14 | Can. Wf. | 19 | D1 |
| Andrews Crosse WC2 | Temple | 65 | C1 |
| Angel All. E1 | Ald. E. | 10 | C2 |
| Angel Ct. EC2 | Bank | 12 | C1 |
| Angel Ct. SW1 | Green Pk. | 34 | D3 |
| Angel Pas. EC4 | Cann. St. | 20 | C4 |
| Angel Pl. SE1 | Boro. | 17 | C2 |
| Angel St. EC1 | St. Paul's | 61 | C2 |
| Angel Wk. W6 | Hamm. | 35 | B3 |
| Angler's La. NW5 | Chalk Fm. | 18 | B1 |
| Annabel Clo. E14 | Can. Wf. | 19 | C1 |
| Ann's Clo. SW1 | Knights. | 40 | C2 |
| Ann's Pl. E1 | Ald. E. | 10 | B1 |
| Ansdell St. W8 | High St. Kens. | 36 | C3 |
| Anselm Rd. SW6 | W. Brom. | 24 | B4 |
| Apothecary St. EC4 | Black. | 15 | B2 |
| Apple Tree Yd. SW1 | Picc. Circ. | 56 | B3 |
| Applegarth Rd. W14 | Olym. | 35 | C1 |
| Appold St. EC2 | Liv. St. | 44 | B1 |
| Apsley Way W1 | Hyde Pk. Cor. | 38 | C2 |
| Aquinas St. SE1 | S'wark | 64 | B2 |
| Arcade, The EC2 | Liv. St. | 44 | B2 |
| Arcadia St. E14 | Can. Wf. | 19 | B1 |
| Arch St. SE1 | El. & Cas. | 26 | C2 |
| Archel Rd. W14 | W. Kens. | 24 | A4 |
| Archer St. W1 | Picc. Circ. | 56 | C1 |
| Archery Clo. W2 | M. Arch | 47 | A2 |
| Archibald Ms. W1 | Bond St. | 16 | C4 |
| Argent St. SE1 | S'wark | 64 | D3 |
| Argyle Pl. W6 | Ravens. Pk. | 35 | A2 |
| Argyle Sq. WC1 | King's X | 39 | C3 |
| Argyle St. WC1 | King's X | 39 | B3 |
| Argyle Wk. WC1 | King's X | 39 | B4 |
| Argyll Rd. W8 | High St. Kens. | 36 | B2 |
| Argyll St. W1 | Ox. Circ. | 54 | C3 |
| Arlington Rd. NW1 | Cam. Tn. | 18 | B3 |
| Arlington St. SW1 | Green Pk. | 34 | C2 |
| Armstrong Rd. SW7 | S. Kens. | 63 | B2 |
| Arne St. WC2 | Cov. Gdn. | 23 | C2 |
| Arneway St. SW1 | St. Jam. Pk. | 60 | D4 |
| Artesian Rd. W2 | Nott. Hill Gate | 52 | C1 |
| Arthur St. EC4 | Mon. | 49 | B2 |
| Artillery La. E1 | Liv. St. | 44 | C2 |
| Artillery Pas. E1 | Liv. St. | 44 | C2 |
| Artillery Pl. SW1 | St. Jam. Pk. | 60 | C4 |
| Artillery Row SW1 | St. Jam. Pk. | 60 | C4 |
| Artizan St. E1 | Ald. | 10 | A2 |
| Arundel Gdns. W11 | Holl. Pk. | 52 | B2 |
| Arundel Great Ct. WC2 | Temple | 65 | B2 |
| Arundel St. WC2 | Temple | 65 | B2 |
| Arundel Ter. SW13 | Ravens. Pk. | 35 | A4 |
| Ashbridge St. NW8 | Edgw. Rd. | 25 | C1 |
| Ashburn Gdns. SW7 | Glos. Rd. | 31 | B2 |
| Ashburn Pl. SW7 | Glos. Rd. | 31 | B2 |
| Ashford St. N1 | Old St. | 53 | D1 |
| Ashland Rd. W1 | Baker St. | 11 | C3 |
| Ashley Gdns. SW1 | St. Jam. Pk. | 60 | B4 |
| Ashley Pl. SW1 | Vic. | 69 | C2 |
| Ashmill St. NW1 | Edgw. Rd. | 25 | C2 |
| Ashton St. E14 | Can. Wf. | 19 | D2 |
| Aske St. N1 | Old St. | 53 | D1 |
| Aspen Gdns. W6 | Ravens. Pk. | 35 | A3 |
| Aspen Way E14 | N. Green. | 51 | B1 |
| Aspenlea Rd. W6 | Bar. Ct. | 35 | C4 |
| Assam St. E1 | Ald. E. | 10 | D2 |
| Aste St. E14 | Can. Wf. | 19 | D4 |
| Astrop Ms. W6 | Hamm. | 35 | B1 |
| Astwood Ms. SW7 | Glos. Rd. | 31 | A2 |
| Atherstone Ms. SW7 | Glos. Rd. | 31 | C2 |
| Athlone St. NW5 | Chalk Fm. | 18 | A1 |
| Athol Sq. E14 | Can. Wf. | 19 | D1 |
| Atlas Rd., Wem. | Wem Pk. | 72 | D3 |
| Atterbury St. SW1 | Pim. | 57 | D2 |
| Atwood Rd. W6 | Ravens. Pk. | 35 | A2 |
| Aubrey Rd. W8 | Holl. Pk. | 52 | B3 |
| Aubrey Wk. W8 | Holl. Pk. | 52 | B3 |
| Auckland St. SE11 | Vaux. | 68 | D2 |
| Augusta St. E14 | Can. Wf. | 19 | C1 |
| Augustine Rd. W14 | Olym. | 35 | C1 |
| Augustus St. NW1 | Morn. Cres. | 18 | B4 |
| Auriol Rd. W14 | Bar. Ct. | 35 | D2 |

| | | | |
|---|---|---|---|
| Austin Friars EC2 | Bank | 12 | C1 |
| Austin Friars Pas. EC2 | Bank | 12 | C1 |
| Austin Friars Sq. EC2 | Bank | 12 | C1 |
| Austral St. SE11 | El. & Cas. | 26 | A3 |
| Ave Maria La. EC4 | Black. | 15 | C2 |
| Averill St. W6 | Bar. Ct. | 35 | C4 |
| Avery Fm. Row SW1 | Vic. | 69 | A4 |
| Avery Row W1 | Ox. Circ. | 54 | B4 |
| Avon Pl. SE1 | Boro. | 17 | B3 |
| Avondale Pk. Gdns. W11 | Lad. Gr. | 52 | A2 |
| Avondale Pk. Rd. W11 | Lad. Gr. | 52 | A2 |
| Avonmore Rd. W14 | Bar. Ct. | 35 | D2 |
| Avonmouth St. SE1 | El. & Cas. | 26 | C1 |
| Aybrook St. W1 | Baker St. | 11 | C4 |
| Aylesbury St. EC1 | Farr. | 30 | C1 |
| Aylesford St. SW1 | Pim. | 57 | B4 |
| Aynhoe Rd. W14 | Hamm. | 35 | C2 |
| Ayres St. SE1 | Boro. | 17 | B2 |
| Ayrton Rd. SW7 | S. Kens. | 63 | B1 |

## B

| | | | |
|---|---|---|---|
| Babmaes St. SW1 | Picc. Circ. | 56 | C3 |
| Baches St. N1 | Old St. | 53 | C2 |
| Back Hill EC1 | Chan. La. | 21 | B1 |
| Baden Pl. SE1 | Boro. | 17 | C2 |
| Bainbridge St. WC1 | Tott. Ct. Rd. | 66 | C3 |
| Baird St. EC1 | Old St. | 53 | A3 |
| Baker St. NW1 | Baker St. | 11 | B2 |
| Baker St. W1 | Baker St. | 11 | B3 |
| Baker's Ms. W1 | M. Arch | 47 | D1 |
| Baker's Row EC1 | Chan. La. | 21 | B1 |
| Balcombe St. NW1 | Mary. | 48 | C1 |
| Balderton St. W1 | Bond St. | 16 | B2 |
| Baldwin St. EC1 | Old St. | 53 | B2 |
| Baldwin's Gdns. EC1 | Chan. La. | 21 | B2 |
| Balfe St. N1 | King's X | 39 | C2 |
| Balfour Pl. W1 | Bond St. | 16 | B4 |
| Balniel Gate SW1 | Pim. | 57 | C3 |
| Baltic St. E. EC1 | Barb. | 13 | C1 |
| Baltic St. W. EC1 | Barb. | 13 | C1 |
| Banbury Ct. WC2 | Leic. Sq. | 43 | C2 |
| Banim St. W6 | Ravens. Pk. | 35 | A2 |
| Bankside SE1 | Mans. Ho. | 46 | B4 |
| Banner St. EC1 | Barb. | 13 | D1 |
| Bannerman Ho. SW8 | Vaux. | 68 | D4 |
| Barb Ms. W6 | Hamm. | 35 | B1 |
| Barbican, The EC2 | Barb. | 13 | C2 |
| Barbon Clo. WC1 | Russ. Sq. | 59 | C3 |
| Barge Ho. St. SE1 | S'wark | 64 | B1 |
| Bark Pl. W2 | Bays. | 14 | B2 |

| | | | |
|---|---|---|---|
| Barker Dr. NW1 | Cam. Tn. | 18 | C2 |
| Barker St. SW10 | W. Brom. | 24 | D4 |
| Barkston Gdns. SW5 | Earls Ct. | 24 | C2 |
| Barley Mow Pas. EC1 | Barb. | 13 | C2 |
| Barleycorn Way E14 | Can. Wf. | 19 | A2 |
| Barlow Pl. W1 | Green Pk. | 34 | B1 |
| Barnaby Pl. SW7 | Glos. Rd. | 31 | D3 |
| Barnard's Inn EC1 | Chan. La. | 21 | B4 |
| Barnby St. NW1 | Euston | 28 | B2 |
| Barnham St. SE1 | London Br. | 45 | D4 |
| Barnhill Rd., Wem. | Wem Pk | 72 | D2 |
| Barons Ct. Rd. W14 | Bar. Ct. | 35 | D3 |
| Barons Keep W14 | Bar. Ct. | 35 | D3 |
| Barons Pl. SE1 | Lamb. N. | 41 | C2 |
| Barrett St. W1 | Bond St. | 16 | B2 |
| Barrie Est. W2 | Lanc. Gate | 42 | B2 |
| Barter St. WC1 | Holb. | 37 | B2 |
| Bartholomew Clo. EC1 | Barb. | 13 | C3 |
| Bartholomew La. EC2 | Bank | 12 | C2 |
| Bartholomew Pl. EC1 | Barb. | 13 | C3 |
| Bartholomew Rd. NW5 | Cam. Tn. | 18 | C1 |
| Bartholomew Sq. EC1 | Old St. | 53 | A3 |
| Bartholomew Vil. NW5 | Cam. Tn. | 18 | C1 |
| Bartle Rd. W11 | Lad. Gr. | 52 | A1 |
| Bartlett Clo. E14 | Can. Wf. | 19 | B1 |
| Bartlett Ct. EC4 | Chan. La. | 21 | C4 |
| Barton Rd. W14 | Bar. Ct. | 35 | D3 |
| Barton St. SW1 | Westmin. | 73 | B4 |
| Basil St. SW3 | Knights. | 40 | B3 |
| Basing Hill, Wem. | Wem Pk. | 72 | A1 |
| Basing St. W11 | Lad. Gr. | 52 | B1 |
| Basinghall Ave. EC2 | Moor. | 50 | B3 |
| Basinghall St. EC2 | Bank | 12 | B1 |
| Bassett St. NW5 | Chalk Fm. | 18 | A1 |
| Bateman St. W1 | Tott. Ct. Rd. | 66 | B4 |
| Bateman's Bldgs. W1 | Tott. Ct. Rd. | 66 | B4 |
| Bath Ct. EC1 | Chan. La. | 21 | B1 |
| Bath St. EC1 | Old St. | 53 | A2 |
| Bath Ter. SE1 | El. & Cas. | 26 | C2 |
| Bathurst Ms. W2 | Lanc. Gate | 42 | C2 |
| Bathurst St. W2 | Lanc. Gate | 42 | C2 |
| Batoum Gdns. W6 | Hamm. | 35 | B1 |
| Battle Bri. La. SE1 | London Br. | 45 | C3 |
| Battle Bri. Rd. NW1 | King's X | 39 | B2 |
| Bayham Pl. NW1 | Cam. Tn. | 18 | C3 |
| Bayham St. NW1 | Cam. Tn. | 18 | C3 |
| Bayley St. WC1 | Goodge St. | 32 | C3 |
| Baylis Rd. SE1 | Lamb. N. | 41 | B2 |

79

| | | | | | | | | |
|---|---|---|---|---|---|---|---|
| Bishops Bri. W2 | Padd. | 55 | A2 | Bolton Gdns. SW5 | Earls Ct. | 24 | C3 |
| Bishops Bri. Rd. W2 | Nott. Hill Gate | 52 | D1 | Bolton Gdns. Ms. SW10 | Glos. Rd. | 31 | A4 |
| Bishop's Ct. EC4 | Black. | 15 | B1 | | | | |
| Bishop's Ct. WC2 | Chan. La. | 21 | B4 | Bolton St. W1 | Green Pk. | 34 | B2 |
| Bishopsgate EC2 | Mon. | 49 | C1 | Boltons, The SW10 | Glos. Rd. | 31 | B4 |
| Bishopsgate Arc. EC2 | Liv. St. | 44 | C2 | Boltons Pl. SW5 | Earls Ct. | 24 | D3 |
| Bishopsgate Chyd. EC2 | Liv. St. | 44 | B3 | Bomore Rd. W11 | Lad. Gr. | 52 | A2 |
| | | | | Bond Ct. EC4 | Bank | 12 | B2 |
| Bittern St. SE1 | Boro. | 17 | A3 | Bondway SW8 | Vaux. | 68 | C3 |
| Black Friars Ct. EC4 | Black. | 15 | B3 | Bonhill St. EC2 | Old St. | 53 | C4 |
| Black Friars La. EC4 | Black. | 15 | B3 | Bonnington Sq. SW8 | Vaux. | 68 | D3 |
| Black Horse Ct. SE1 | Boro. | 17 | D4 | Bonny St. NW1 | Cam. Tn. | 18 | C2 |
| Black Swan Yd. SE1 | London Br. | 45 | C4 | Book Ms. WC2 | Tott. Ct. Rd. | 66 | C4 |
| Blackall St. EC2 | Old St. | 53 | D3 | Boord St. SE10 | N. Green. | 51 | C4 |
| Blackbird Hill NW9 | Wem Pk. | 72 | D1 | Boot St. N1 | Old St. | 53 | D2 |
| Blackburne's Ms. W1 | M. Arch | 47 | D3 | Booth's Pl. W1 | Goodge St. | 32 | B3 |
| Blackfriars Bri. EC4 | Black. | 15 | B4 | Borer's Pas. E1 | Ald. | 10 | A2 |
| Blackfriars Bri. SE1 | Black. | 15 | B4 | Borough High St. (N) SE1 | London Br. | 45 | A4 |
| Blackfriars Pas. EC4 | Black. | 15 | B3 | | | | |
| Blackfriars Rd. SE1 | S'wark | 64 | C1 | Borough High St. (Cen) SE1 | Boro. | 17 | B3 |
| Blacklands Ter. SW3 | Sloane Sq. | 62 | A3 | | | | |
| Blackwall Pier E14 | N. Green. | 51 | C1 | Borough Rd. SE1 | El. & Cas. | 26 | B1 |
| Blackwall Tunnel E14 | N. Green. | 51 | B2 | Borough Sq. SE1 | Boro. | 17 | A3 |
| | | | | Boscobel Pl. SW1 | Sloane Sq. | 62 | D2 |
| Blackwall Tunnel App. SE10 | N. Green. | 51 | C3 | Boscobel St. NW8 | Edgw. Rd. | 25 | B1 |
| | | | | Boston Pl. NW1 | Mary. | 48 | C2 |
| Blackwall Way E14 | Can. Wf. | 19 | D2 | Boswell Ct. WC1 | Russ. Sq. | 59 | C3 |
| Blair St. E14 | Can. Wf. | 19 | D1 | Boswell St. WC1 | Russ. Sq. | 59 | C3 |
| Blandford Sq. NW1 | Mary. | 48 | B2 | Botolph All. EC3 | Mon. | 49 | C2 |
| Blandford St. W1 | M. Arch | 47 | C1 | Botolph La. EC3 | Mon. | 49 | C2 |
| Bleeding Heart Yd. EC1 | Chan. La. | 21 | C3 | Botts Ms. W2 | Bays. | 14 | A1 |
| | | | | Botts Pas. W2 | Bays. | 14 | A1 |
| Blenheim Cres. W11 | Lad. Gr. | 52 | A2 | Boundary Row SE1 | S'wark | 64 | C3 |
| Blenheim St. W1 | Bond St. | 16 | C2 | Bourchier St. W1 | Picc. Circ. | 56 | C1 |
| Blithfield St. W8 | High St. Kens. | 36 | C3 | Bourdon Pl. W1 | Ox. Circ. | 54 | B4 |
| Blomfield St. EC2 | Moor. | 50 | C3 | Bourdon St. W1 | Bond St. | 16 | C4 |
| Bloomburg St. SW1 | Pim. | 57 | A2 | Bourlet Clo. W1 | Goodge St. | 32 | A3 |
| Bloomfield Pl. W1 | Ox. Circ. | 54 | B4 | Bourne Est. EC1 | Chan. La. | 21 | B2 |
| Bloomfield Ter. SW1 | Sloane Sq. | 62 | D4 | Bourne St. SW1 | Sloane Sq. | 62 | C3 |
| Bloomsbury Ct. WC1 | Holb. | 37 | B2 | Bouverie Pl. W2 | Padd. | 55 | C2 |
| Bloomsbury Pl. WC1 | Russ. Sq. | 59 | C3 | Bouverie St. EC4 | Black. | 15 | A2 |
| Bloomsbury Sq. WC1 | Holb. | 37 | B2 | Bow Chyd. EC4 | Mans. Ho. | 46 | C2 |
| Bloomsbury St. WC1 | Tott. Ct. Rd. | 66 | C2 | Bow La. EC4 | Mans. Ho. | 46 | C2 |
| Bloomsbury Way WC1 | Tott. Ct. Rd. | 66 | D3 | Bow St. WC2 | Cov. Gdn. | 23 | C2 |
| Blore Ct. W1 | Picc. Circ. | 56 | C1 | Bowen St. E14 | Can. Wf. | 19 | C1 |
| Blue Anchor Yd. E1 | Ald. E. | 10 | D4 | Bowfell Rd. W6 | Hamm. | 35 | B4 |
| Blue Ball Yd. SW1 | Green Pk. | 34 | C3 | Bowland Yd. SW1 | Knights. | 40 | C2 |
| Blythe Rd. W14 | Olym. | 35 | C1 | Bowling Grn. Pl. SE1 | Boro. | 17 | C2 |
| Bolingbroke Rd. W14 | Olym. | 35 | C1 | Bowling Grn. Wk. N1 | Old St. | 53 | D1 |
| Bolsover St. W1 | Gt. Port. St. | 33 | C3 | Bowman Ave. E16 | N. Green. | 51 | D1 |
| Bolt Ct. EC4 | Black. | 15 | A2 | Bowmans Ms. E1 | Ald. E. | 10 | D4 |

| Boyce St. SE1 | Embk. | 27 | C4 |
| Boyfield St. SE1 | S'wark | 64 | D4 |
| Boyle St. W1 | Ox. Circ. | 54 | C4 |
| Boyne Ter. Ms. W11 | Holl. Pk. | 52 | B3 |
| Brabant Ct. EC3 | Mon. | 49 | C2 |
| Brabazon St. E14 | Can. Wf. | 19 | C1 |
| Brackenbury Gdns. W6 | Ravens. Pk. | 35 | A1 |
| Brackenbury Rd. W6 | Ravens. Pk. | 35 | A1 |
| Brackley St. EC1 | Barb. | 13 | D2 |
| Brad St. SE1 | S'wark | 64 | B2 |
| Bradmore Pk. Rd. W6 | Ravens. Pk. | 35 | A2 |
| Braham St. E1 | Ald. E. | 10 | C3 |
| Braidwood St. SE1 | London Br. | 45 | C3 |
| Bramber Rd. W14 | W. Kens. | 24 | A4 |
| Bramham Gdns. SW5 | Earls Ct. | 24 | C3 |
| Brandon St. SE17 | El. & Cas. | 26 | D4 |
| Bray Dr. E16 | N. Green. | 51 | D1 |
| Bray Pl. SW3 | Sloane Sq. | 62 | A3 |
| Bread St. EC4 | Mans. Ho. | 46 | C3 |
| Bream's Bldgs. EC4 | Chan. La. | 21 | B4 |
| Brechin Pl. SW7 | Glos. Rd. | 31 | C3 |
| Brecon Rd. W6 | Bar. Ct. | 35 | D4 |
| Bremner Rd. SW7 | S. Kens. | 63 | A1 |
| Brendon St. W1 | Edgw. Rd. | 25 | D4 |
| Brent Grn. Wk., Wem. | Wem Pk. | 72 | D2 |
| Bressenden Pl. SW1 | Vic. | 69 | B1 |
| Brewer St. W1 | Picc. Circ. | 56 | B1 |
| Brewer's Grn. SW1 | St. Jam. Pk. | 60 | B3 |
| Brewers Hall Gdns. EC2 | Moor. | 50 | A3 |
| Brewster Ho. E14 | Can. Wf. | 19 | A2 |
| Brick Ct. EC4 | Temple | 65 | C1 |
| Brick St. W1 | Green Pk. | 34 | A3 |
| Bride Ct. EC4 | Black. | 15 | B2 |
| Bride La. EC4 | Black. | 15 | B2 |
| Bridewell Pl. EC4 | Black. | 15 | B2 |
| Bridford Ms. W1 | Gt. Port. St. | 33 | C4 |
| Bridge App. NW1 | Chalk Fm. | 18 | A2 |
| Bridge Ave. W6 | Ravens. Pk. | 35 | A4 |
| Bridge Pl. SW1 | Vic. | 69 | B3 |
| Bridge Rd., Wem. | Wem Pk. | 72 | B2 |
| Bridge St. SW1 | Westmin. | 73 | B3 |
| Bridge Vw. W6 | Hamm. | 35 | B3 |
| Bridge Yd. SE1 | London Br. | 45 | B2 |
| Bridgefoot SE1 | Vaux. | 68 | C2 |
| Bridgewater Sq. EC2 | Barb. | 13 | C2 |
| Bridgewater St. EC2 | Barb. | 13 | C2 |
| Bridgeway St. NW1 | Euston | 28 | B1 |
| Bridle La. W1 | Picc. Circ. | 56 | B1 |
| Bright St. E14 | Can. Wf. | 19 | C1 |
| Brightlingsea Pl. E14 | Can. Wf. | 19 | A2 |
| Brill Pl. NW1 | King's X | 39 | A2 |
| Brinton Wk. SE1 | S'wark | 64 | C2 |
| Briset St. EC1 | Farr. | 30 | C2 |
| Britannia St. WC1 | King's X | 39 | D3 |
| Britannia Wk. N1 | Old St. | 53 | B1 |
| Britton St. EC1 | Farr. | 30 | C1 |
| Broad Ct. WC2 | Cov. Gdn. | 23 | C2 |
| Broad La. EC2 | Liv. St. | 44 | B2 |
| Broad Sanctuary SW1 | St. Jam. Pk. | 60 | D2 |
| Broad St. Ave. EC2 | Liv. St. | 44 | B2 |
| Broad St. Pl. EC2 | Moor. | 50 | C3 |
| Broad Wk. NW1 | Cam. Tn. | 18 | A4 |
| Broad Wk., The W8 | High St. Kens. | 36 | D1 |
| Broad Yd. EC1 | Farr. | 30 | C1 |
| Broadbent St. W1 | Bond St. | 16 | C3 |
| Broadgate Circle EC2 | Liv. St. | 44 | B1 |
| Broadley St. NW8 | Edgw. Rd. | 25 | B2 |
| Broadley Ter. NW1 | Mary. | 48 | B2 |
| Broadstone Pl. W1 | Baker St. | 11 | C4 |
| Broadwall SE1 | S'wark | 64 | B1 |
| Broadway SW1 | St. Jam. Pk. | 60 | C3 |
| Broadwick St. W1 | Picc. Circ. | 56 | B1 |
| Brockham St. SE1 | Boro. | 17 | B4 |
| Broken Wf. EC4 | Mans. Ho. | 46 | B3 |
| Bromley Pl. W1 | Goodge St. | 32 | A2 |
| Brompton Arc. SW3 | Knights. | 40 | B2 |
| Brompton Pk. Cres. SW6 | W. Brom. | 24 | C4 |
| Brompton Pl. SW3 | Knights. | 40 | A3 |
| Brompton Rd. SW1 | Knights. | 40 | B2 |
| Brompton Rd. SW3 | S. Kens. | 63 | D3 |
| Brompton Rd. SW7 | S. Kens. | 63 | D2 |
| Brompton Sq. SW3 | S. Kens. | 63 | D1 |
| Brook Ave., Wem. | Wem Pk. | 72 | B2 |
| Brook Dr. SE11 | Lamb. N. | 41 | C4 |
| Brook Gate W1 | M. Arch | 47 | C4 |
| Brook Grn. W6 | Hamm. | 35 | B1 |
| Brook Ms. N. W2 | Lanc. Gate | 42 | A2 |
| Brook St. W1 | Bond St. | 16 | C3 |
| Brook St. W2 | Lanc. Gate | 42 | C2 |
| Brooke St. EC1 | Chan. La. | 21 | B3 |
| Brooke's Ct. EC1 | Chan. La. | 21 | B2 |
| Brookes Mkt. EC1 | Chan. La. | 21 | B2 |
| Brook's Ms. W1 | Bond St. | 16 | C3 |
| Brown Hart Gdns. W1 | Bond St. | 16 | B3 |
| Brown St. W1 | M. Arch | 47 | B1 |
| Brownfield St. E14 | Can. Wf. | 19 | C1 |
| Browning Ms. W1 | Reg. Pk. | 58 | A4 |
| Brownlow Ms. WC1 | Chan. La. | 21 | A1 |

| | | |
|---|---|---|
| Brownlow St. WC1 | Chan. La. | 21 A3 |
| Brown's Bldgs. EC3 | Ald. | 10 A3 |
| Brune St. E1 | Ald. E. | 10 B1 |
| Bruno Pl. NW9 | Wem Pk. | 72 D1 |
| Brunswick Cen. WC1 | Russ. Sq. | 59 B1 |
| Brunswick Ct. SE1 | London Br. | 45 D4 |
| Brunswick Gdns. W8 | Nott. Hill Gate | 52 C3 |
| Brunswick Ms. W1 | M. Arch | 47 C1 |
| Brunswick Pl. N1 | Old St. | 53 C2 |
| Brunswick Sq. WC1 | Russ. Sq. | 59 C1 |
| Brushfield St. E1 | Liv. St. | 44 C1 |
| Bruton La. W1 | Green Pk. | 34 B1 |
| Bruton Pl. W1 | Green Pk. | 34 B1 |
| Bruton St. W1 | Green Pk. | 34 B1 |
| Bryan Rd. SE16 | Can. Wf. | 19 A4 |
| Bryanston Ms. E. W1 | Mary. | 48 C4 |
| Bryanston Ms. W. W1 | Mary. | 48 C4 |
| Bryanston Pl. W1 | Mary. | 48 C4 |
| Bryanston Sq. W1 | Mary. | 48 C4 |
| Bryanston St. W1 | M. Arch | 47 B2 |
| Brydges St. WC2 | Char. X | 22 B2 |
| Buck Hill Wk. W2 | Lanc. Gate | 42 C3 |
| Buck St. NW1 | Cam. Tn. | 18 B2 |
| Buckingham Arc. WC2 | Char. X | 22 C2 |
| Buckingham Gate SW1 | St. Jam. Pk. | 60 A2 |
| Buckingham Ms. SW1 | Vic. | 69 C1 |
| Buckingham Palace Rd. SW1 | Vic. | 69 A4 |
| Buckingham Pl. SW1 | Vic. | 69 C1 |
| Buckingham St. WC2 | Char. X | 22 C2 |
| Buckle St. E1 | Ald. E. | 10 C2 |
| Bucklersbury EC4 | Bank | 12 B2 |
| Buckley St. SE1 | Embk. | 27 C4 |
| Bucknall St. WC2 | Tott. Ct. Rd. | 66 C3 |
| Buddings Circle, Wem. | Wem Pk. | 72 D2 |
| Budge Row EC4 | Cann. St. | 20 C3 |
| Budge's Wk. W2 | Queens. | 14 D4 |
| Bulinga St. SW1 | Pim. | 57 D2 |
| Bull Inn Ct. WC2 | Char. X | 22 C2 |
| Bull Wf. La. EC4 | Mans. Ho. | 46 C3 |
| Bullied Way SW1 | Vic. | 69 B4 |
| Bullivant St. E14 | Can. Wf. | 19 D1 |
| Bull's Head Pas. EC3 | Mon. | 49 C1 |
| Bulmer Pl. W11 | Nott. Hill Gate | 52 C3 |
| Bulstrode Pl. W1 | Reg. Pk. | 58 A4 |
| Bulstrode St. W1 | Bond St. | 16 B1 |
| Bunhill Row EC1 | Old St. | 53 B3 |
| Bunhouse Pl. SW1 | Sloane Sq. | 62 C4 |
| Buonaparte Ms. SW1 | Pim. | 57 B3 |
| Burcham St. E14 | Can. Wf. | 19 C1 |
| Burdett St. SE1 | Lamb. N. | 41 B3 |
| Burgon St. EC4 | Black. | 15 C2 |
| Burleigh St. WC2 | Cov. Gdn. | 23 C3 |
| Burlington Arc. W1 | Green Pk. | 34 C1 |
| Burlington Gdns. W1 | Green Pk. | 34 C1 |
| Burne Jones Ho. W14 | W. Kens. | 24 A2 |
| Burne St. NW1 | Edgw. Rd. | 25 C2 |
| Burrell St. SE1 | S'wark | 64 C1 |
| Burrows Ms. SE1 | S'wark | 64 C1 |
| Burton Ms. SW1 | Sloane Sq. | 62 D3 |
| Burton Pl. WC1 | Euston | 28 D3 |
| Burton St. WC1 | Euston | 28 D3 |
| Burwash Ho. SE1 | Boro. | 17 D3 |
| Burwood Pl. W2 | Edgw. Rd. | 25 D4 |
| Bury Ct. EC3 | Ald. | 10 A2 |
| Bury Pl. WC1 | Tott. Ct. Rd. | 66 D2 |
| Bury St. EC3 | Ald. | 10 A3 |
| Bury St. SW1 | Green Pk. | 34 C2 |
| Bury Wk. SW3 | S. Kens. | 63 D4 |
| Busby Ms. NW5 | Cam. Tn. | 18 D1 |
| Busby Pl. NW5 | Cam. Tn. | 18 D1 |
| Bush La. EC4 | Cann. St. | 20 C3 |
| Bute Gdns. W6 | Hamm. | 35 C2 |
| Bute St. SW7 | S. Kens. | 63 B3 |
| Butler Pl. SW1 | St. Jam. Pk. | 60 C3 |
| Butterwick W6 | Hamm. | 35 B2 |
| Buttesland St. N1 | Old St. | 53 C1 |
| Buxton Ct. N1 | Old St. | 53 A1 |
| Bygrove St. E14 | Can. Wf. | 19 C1 |
| Byng Pl. WC1 | Goodge St. | 32 C1 |
| Byng St. E14 | Can. Wf. | 19 B4 |
| Byward St. EC3 | T. Hill | 67 B3 |
| Bywater St. SW3 | Sloane Sq. | 62 A4 |
| Bywell Pl. W1 | Goodge St. | 32 A3 |

## C

| | | |
|---|---|---|
| Cabbell St. NW1 | Edgw. Rd. | 25 C3 |
| Cabot Sq. E14 | Can. Wf. | 19 B3 |
| Cadogan Gdns. SW3 | Sloane Sq. | 62 B2 |
| Cadogan Gate SW1 | Sloane Sq. | 62 B2 |
| Cadogan La. SW1 | Sloane Sq. | 62 C1 |
| Cadogan Pl. SW1 | Knights. | 40 C3 |
| Cadogan Sq. SW1 | Knights. | 40 C4 |
| Cadogan St. SW3 | Sloane Sq. | 62 A3 |
| Cahill St. EC1 | Barb. | 13 D1 |
| Caithness Rd. W14 | Olym. | 35 C2 |
| Caleb St. SE1 | Boro. | 17 A2 |
| Caledonia St. N1 | King's X | 39 C2 |
| Caledonian Rd. N1 | King's X | 39 C2 |
| Callendar Rd. SW7 | S. Kens. | 63 B1 |

| | | | | | | | |
|---|---|---|---|---|---|---|---|
| Calshot St. N1 | King's X | 39 | D1 | Carbis Rd. E14 | Can. Wf. | 19 | A1 |
| Calvert's Bldgs. SE1 | London Br. | 45 | A3 | Carburton St. W1 | Gt. Port. St. | 33 | C4 |
| Cambridge Circ. WC2 | Tott. Ct. Rd. | 66 | C4 | Cardington St. NW1 | Euston | 28 | B2 |
| Cambridge Clo. NW10 | Wem Pk. | 72 | D2 | Cardross St. W6 | Ravens. Pk. | 35 | A1 |
| Cambridge Gate NW1 | Gt. Port. St. | 33 | C2 | Carey La. EC2 | St. Paul's | 61 | C2 |
| Cambridge Gate Ms. NW1 | Gt. Port. St. | 33 | C2 | Carey Pl. SW1 | Pim. | 57 | B2 |
| Cambridge Gro. W6 | Ravens. Pk. | 35 | A2 | Carey St. WC2 | Temple | 65 | B1 |
| Cambridge Pl. W8 | High St. Kens. | 36 | C2 | Carlisle Ave. EC3 | Ald. | 10 | B3 |
| Cambridge Sq. W2 | Edgw. Rd. | 25 | C4 | Carlisle La. SE1 | Lamb. N. | 41 | A4 |
| Cambridge Ter. NW1 | Gt. Port. St. | 33 | B1 | Carlisle Ms. NW8 | Edgw. Rd. | 25 | B2 |
| Cambridge Ter. Ms. NW1 | Gt. Port. St. | 33 | C1 | Carlisle Pl. SW1 | Vic. | 69 | C2 |
| | | | | Carlisle St. W1 | Tott. Ct. Rd. | 66 | B4 |
| Camden High St. NW1 | Cam. Tn. | 18 | B3 | Carlos Pl. W1 | Bond St. | 16 | B3 |
| Camden La. N7 | Cam. Tn. | 18 | D1 | Carlton Gdns. SW1 | Picc. Circ. | 56 | C4 |
| Camden Ms. NW1 | Cam. Tn. | 18 | C2 | Carlton Ho. Ter. SW1 | Picc. Circ. | 56 | C4 |
| Camden Pk. Rd. NW1 | Cam. Tn. | 18 | D1 | Carlton St. SW1 | Picc. Circ. | 56 | C2 |
| Camden Rd. NW1 | Cam. Tn. | 18 | C2 | Carlton Twr. Pl. SW1 | Knights. | 40 | C3 |
| Camden Sq. NW1 | Cam. Tn. | 18 | D1 | Carmel Ct., Wem. | Wem Pk. | 72 | C1 |
| Camden St. NW1 | Cam. Tn. | 18 | C2 | Carmen St. E14 | Can. Wf. | 19 | C1 |
| Camley St. NW1 | King's X | 39 | A1 | Carnaby St. W1 | Ox. Circ. | 54 | C3 |
| Camomile St. E1 | Liv. St. | 44 | B3 | Carol St. NW1 | Cam. Tn. | 18 | C3 |
| Campden Gro. W8 | High St. Kens. | 36 | B2 | Caroline Clo. W2 | Queens. | 14 | C3 |
| Campden Hill W8 | High St. Kens. | 36 | B2 | Caroline Pl. W2 | Bays. | 14 | C2 |
| Campden Hill Gdns. W8 | Nott. Hill Gate | 52 | C3 | Caroline Pl. Ms. W2 | Queens. | 14 | C3 |
| | | | | Caroline Ter. SW1 | Sloane Sq. | 62 | C3 |
| Campden Hill Rd. W8 | Nott. Hill Gate | 52 | C3 | Carpenter St. W1 | Bond St. | 16 | C4 |
| Campden Hill Sq. W8 | Holl. Pk. | 52 | B3 | Carrington St. W1 | Green Pk. | 34 | A3 |
| Campden St. W8 | Nott. Hill Gate | 52 | C3 | Carron Clo. E14 | Can. Wf. | 19 | C1 |
| Camperdown St. E1 | Ald. E. | 10 | C3 | Carter La. EC4 | Black. | 15 | C2 |
| Canada Sq. E14 | Can. Wf. | 19 | C3 | Carteret St. SW1 | St. Jam. Pk. | 60 | C2 |
| Canary Wf. E14 | Can. Wf. | 19 | B3 | Carthew Rd. W6 | Ravens. Pk. | 35 | A1 |
| Candover St. W1 | Goodge St. | 32 | A3 | Carthew Vil. W6 | Ravens. Pk. | 35 | A1 |
| Canning Pl. W8 | High St. Kens. | 36 | D3 | Carthusian St. EC1 | Barb. | 13 | C2 |
| Cannon Dr. E14 | Can. Wf. | 19 | B2 | Cartier Circle E14 | Can. Wf. | 19 | C3 |
| Cannon St. (W) EC4 | St. Paul's | 61 | C3 | Carting La. WC2 | Char. X | 22 | C2 |
| Cannon St. (Cen) EC4 | Cann. St. | 20 | A2 | Carton St. W1 | M. Arch | 47 | C1 |
| Cannon St. (Cen) EC4 | Mans. Ho. | 46 | B2 | Cartwright Gdns. WC1 | King's X | 39 | B4 |
| Cannon St. (E) EC4 | Mon. | 49 | A2 | Cartwright St. E1 | T. Hill | 67 | D3 |
| Canon Row SW1 | Westmin. | 73 | B2 | Casson St. E1 | Ald. E. | 10 | D1 |
| Canon Trd. Est., The, Wem. | Wem Pk. | 72 | C3 | Castle Baynard St. EC4 | Black. | 15 | C3 |
| Cantelowes Rd. NW1 | Cam. Tn. | 18 | D1 | Castle Ct. EC3 | Bank | 12 | C2 |
| Canterbury Pl. SE17 | El. & Cas. | 26 | B4 | Castle La. SW1 | Vic. | 69 | C1 |
| Canton St. E14 | Can. Wf. | 19 | B1 | Castle Rd. NW1 | Chalk Fm. | 18 | B2 |
| Canvey St. SE1 | S'wark | 64 | D1 | Castle Yd. SE1 | S'wark | 64 | D1 |
| Capel Ct. EC2 | Bank | 12 | C2 | Castlehaven Rd. NW1 | Cam. Tn. | 18 | B2 |
| Capener's Clo. SW1 | Hyde Pk. Cor. | 38 | B3 | | | | |
| Capper St. WC1 | Warr. St. | 70 | C3 | Castlereagh St. W1 | Edgw. Rd. | 25 | D4 |
| Capstan Sq. E14 | Can. Wf. | 19 | D4 | Castletown Rd. W14 | Bar. Ct. | 35 | D3 |
| Caradoc Clo. W2 | Nott. Hill Gate | 52 | C1 | | | | |

| | | | |
|---|---|---|---|
| Clifton St. EC2 | Liv. St. | 44 | B1 |
| Clink St. SE1 | London Br. | 45 | A2 |
| Clipstone Ms. W1 | Warr. St. | 70 | B3 |
| Clipstone St. W1 | Gt. Port. St. | 33 | C4 |
| Cliveden Pl. SW1 | Sloane Sq. | 62 | C2 |
| Cloak La. EC4 | Cann. St. | 20 | C3 |
| Close, The (Barnhill Road), Wem. | Wem Pk. | 72 | D2 |
| Cloth Ct. EC1 | Barb. | 13 | B3 |
| Cloth Fair EC1 | Barb. | 13 | B3 |
| Cloth St. EC1 | Barb. | 13 | C2 |
| Clothier St. E1 | Ald. | 10 | A2 |
| Clove Cres. E14 | N. Green. | 51 | B1 |
| Cluny Ms. SW5 | Earls Ct. | 24 | B2 |
| Clydesdale Rd. W11 | Lad. Gr. | 52 | B1 |
| Coach & Horses Yd. W1 | Ox. Circ. | 54 | C4 |
| Cobb St. E1 | Ald. E. | 10 | B1 |
| Cobourg St. NW1 | Euston Sq. | 29 | B2 |
| Coburg Clo. SW1 | Vic. | 69 | D3 |
| Cock Hill E1 | Liv. St. | 44 | C2 |
| Cock La. EC1 | Farr. | 30 | C3 |
| Cockpit Steps SW1 | St. Jam. Pk. | 60 | D2 |
| Cockpit Yd. WC1 | Chan. La. | 21 | A2 |
| Cockspur Ct. SW1 | Char. X | 22 | A3 |
| Cockspur St. SW1 | Char. X | 22 | A3 |
| Cofers Circle, Wem. | Wem Pk. | 72 | C2 |
| Coin St. SE1 | Water. | 71 | C1 |
| Coity Rd. NW5 | Chalk Fm. | 18 | A1 |
| Coke St. E1 | Ald. E. | 10 | D2 |
| Colbeck Ms. SW7 | Glos. Rd. | 31 | A3 |
| Colchester St. E1 | Ald. E. | 10 | C2 |
| Cold Harbour E14 | Can. Wf. | 19 | D4 |
| Cole St. SE1 | Boro. | 17 | B3 |
| Coleherne Ct. SW5 | Earls Ct. | 24 | C3 |
| Coleherne Ms. SW10 | Earls Ct. | 24 | C3 |
| Coleherne Rd. SW10 | Earls Ct. | 24 | C3 |
| Coleman St. EC2 | Bank | 12 | B1 |
| Colet Gdns. W14 | Bar. Ct. | 35 | C3 |
| Coley St. WC1 | Chan. La. | 21 | A1 |
| College Hill EC4 | Mans. Ho. | 46 | C3 |
| College Ms. SW1 | Westmin. | 73 | B4 |
| College Pl. NW1 | Cam. Tn. | 18 | C3 |
| College St. EC4 | Cann. St. | 20 | C3 |
| Collier St. N1 | King's X | 39 | D2 |
| Collingham Gdns. SW5 | Glos. Rd. | 31 | A3 |
| Collingham Pl. SW5 | Earls Ct. | 24 | C2 |
| Collingham Rd. SW5 | Glos. Rd. | 31 | A2 |
| Collinson St. SE1 | Boro. | 17 | A3 |
| Collinson Wk. SE1 | Boro. | 17 | A3 |

| | | | |
|---|---|---|---|
| Colnbrook St. SE1 | El. & Cas. | 26 | A2 |
| Colombo St. SE1 | S'wark | 64 | C2 |
| Colonnade WC1 | Russ. Sq. | 59 | C2 |
| Colonnade Wk. SW1 | Vic. | 69 | A4 |
| Colville Gdns. W11 | Lad. Gr. | 52 | B1 |
| Colville Hos. W11 | Lad. Gr. | 52 | B1 |
| Colville Pl. W1 | Goodge St. | 32 | B3 |
| Colville Rd. W11 | Lad. Gr. | 52 | B1 |
| Colville Sq. W11 | Lad. Gr. | 52 | B1 |
| Colville Ter. W11 | Lad. Gr. | 52 | B1 |
| Colwith Rd. W6 | Hamm. | 35 | B4 |
| Colworth Gro. SE17 | El. & Cas. | 26 | D4 |
| Comeragh Rd. W14 | Bar. Ct. | 35 | D3 |
| Commercial Rd. E1 | Ald. E. | 10 | D2 |
| Commodity Quay E1 | T. Hill | 67 | D3 |
| Compton Clo. NW1 | Gt. Port. St. | 33 | C4 |
| Compton Pl. WC1 | Russ. Sq. | 59 | B1 |
| Conant Ms. E1 | Ald. E. | 10 | D4 |
| Concert Hall App. SE1 | Water. | 71 | B2 |
| Conduit Ct. WC2 | Leic. Sq. | 43 | C3 |
| Conduit Ms. W2 | Padd. | 55 | B3 |
| Conduit Pas. W2 | Padd. | 55 | B3 |
| Conduit Pl. W2 | Padd. | 55 | B3 |
| Conduit St. W1 | Ox. Circ. | 54 | B4 |
| Connaught Clo. W2 | Padd. | 55 | D3 |
| Connaught Ms. W2 | M. Arch | 47 | B2 |
| Connaught Pl. W2 | M. Arch | 47 | B2 |
| Connaught Sq. W2 | M. Arch | 47 | B2 |
| Connaught St. W2 | M. Arch | 47 | A2 |
| Cons St. SE1 | S'wark | 64 | B3 |
| Constitution Hill SW1 | Hyde Pk. Cor. | 38 | D2 |
| Content St. SE17 | El. & Cas. | 26 | D4 |
| Conway Ms. W1 | Warr. St. | 70 | B3 |
| Conway St. W1 | Warr. St. | 70 | B3 |
| Coomer Pl. SW6 | W. Kens. | 24 | A4 |
| Cooper Clo. SE1 | Lamb. N. | 41 | C2 |
| Coopers La. NW1 | King's X | 39 | A2 |
| Cooper's Row EC3 | T. Hill | 67 | C2 |
| Cope Pl. W8 | High St. Kens. | 36 | B3 |
| Copenhagen Pl. E14 | Can. Wf. | 19 | A1 |
| Copperfield St. SE1 | S'wark | 64 | D3 |
| Copthall Ave. EC2 | Bank | 12 | C1 |
| Copthall Bldgs. EC2 | Bank | 12 | C1 |
| Copthall Clo. EC2 | Bank | 12 | B1 |
| Coptic St. WC1 | Tott. Ct. Rd. | 66 | D2 |
| Coral St. SE1 | Lamb. N. | 41 | C2 |
| Coram St. WC1 | Russ. Sq. | 59 | B2 |
| Corbet Ct. EC3 | Bank | 12 | C2 |
| Corbet Pl. E1 | Liv. St. | 44 | D1 |
| Cordelia St. E14 | Can. Wf. | 19 | C1 |
| Corinium Clo., Wem. | Wem Pk. | 72 | A3 |

| | | | |
|---|---|---|---|
| Cork St. W1 | Green Pk. | 34 | C1 |
| Cork St. Ms. W1 | Green Pk. | 34 | C1 |
| Corlett St. NW1 | Edgw. Rd. | 25 | C2 |
| Corner Ho. St. WC2 | Char. X | 22 | B3 |
| Cornhill EC3 | Bank | 12 | C2 |
| Cornwall Cres. W11 | Lad. Gr. | 52 | A1 |
| Cornwall Gdns. SW7 | Glos. Rd. | 31 | A1 |
| Cornwall Gdns. Wk. SW7 | Glos. Rd. | 31 | A1 |
| Cornwall Ms. S. SW7 | Glos. Rd. | 31 | B1 |
| Cornwall Ms. W. SW7 | Glos. Rd. | 31 | A1 |
| Cornwall Rd. SE1 | Water. | 71 | C1 |
| Cornwall Ter. NW1 | Baker St. | 11 | B2 |
| Cornwall Ter. Ms. NW1 | Baker St. | 11 | B2 |
| Coronet St. N1 | Old St. | 53 | D2 |
| Corringham Rd., Wem. | Wem Pk. | 72 | B1 |
| Corsham St. N1 | Old St. | 53 | C2 |
| Cosmo Pl. WC1 | Russ. Sq. | 59 | C3 |
| Cosser St. SE1 | Lamb. N. | 41 | B3 |
| Cosway St. NW1 | Mary. | 48 | B3 |
| Cotall St. E14 | Can. Wf. | 19 | B1 |
| Cotham St. SE17 | El. & Cas. | 26 | D4 |
| Cottage Pl. SW3 | S. Kens. | 63 | D2 |
| Cottage St. E14 | Can. Wf. | 19 | C2 |
| Cottesmore Gdns. W8 | High St. Kens. | 36 | C3 |
| Cotton St. E14 | Can. Wf. | 19 | D2 |
| Cottons La. SE1 | London Br. | 45 | B2 |
| Coulson St. SW3 | Sloane Sq. | 62 | A4 |
| Coulter Rd. W6 | Ravens. Pk. | 35 | A1 |
| Counter Ct. SE1 | London Br. | 45 | A3 |
| Counter St. SE1 | London Br. | 45 | C3 |
| County St. SE1 | El. & Cas. | 26 | D2 |
| Courtfield Gdns. SW5 | Glos. Rd. | 31 | A3 |
| Courtfield Ms. SW5 | Glos. Rd. | 31 | A3 |
| Courtfield Rd. SW7 | Glos. Rd. | 31 | B2 |
| Courtnell St. W2 | Nott. Hill Gate | 52 | C1 |
| Cousin La. EC4 | Cann. St. | 20 | C4 |
| Covent Gdn. WC2 | Cov. Gdn. | 23 | C3 |
| Coventry St. W1 | Picc. Circ. | 56 | C2 |
| Cowcross St. EC1 | Farr. | 30 | C2 |
| Cowley St. SW1 | Westmin. | 73 | B4 |
| Cowper St. EC2 | Old St. | 53 | C3 |
| Crace St. NW1 | Euston | 28 | C2 |
| Craigs Ct. SW1 | Char. X | 22 | B3 |
| Cramer St. W1 | Reg. Pk. | 58 | A4 |
| Cramond Clo. W6 | Bar. Ct. | 35 | D4 |
| Crampton St. SE17 | El. & Cas. | 26 | C4 |
| Cranbourn All. WC2 | Leic. Sq. | 43 | B2 |
| Cranbourn St. WC2 | Leic. Sq. | 43 | B2 |
| Crane Ct. EC4 | Black. | 15 | A2 |
| Cranfield Row SE1 | Lamb. N. | 41 | C3 |
| Cranleigh St. NW1 | Euston | 28 | B1 |
| Cranley Gdns. SW7 | Glos. Rd. | 31 | C4 |
| Cranley Ms. SW7 | Glos. Rd. | 31 | C4 |
| Cranley Pl. SW7 | Glos. Rd. | 31 | D3 |
| Cranwood St. EC1 | Old St. | 53 | C2 |
| Craven Hill W2 | Lanc. Gate | 42 | A2 |
| Craven Hill Gdns. W2 | Bays. | 14 | D2 |
| Craven Hill Ms. W2 | Lanc. Gate | 42 | A2 |
| Craven Pas. WC2 | Char. X | 22 | B3 |
| Craven Rd. W2 | Lanc. Gate | 42 | A2 |
| Craven St. WC2 | Char. X | 22 | B3 |
| Craven Ter. W2 | Lanc. Gate | 42 | A2 |
| Crawford Ms. W1 | Mary. | 48 | C4 |
| Crawford Pas. EC1 | Chan. La. | 21 | B1 |
| Crawford Pl. W1 | Edgw. Rd. | 25 | D4 |
| Crawford St. W1 | Edgw. Rd. | 25 | D3 |
| Creechurch La. EC3 | Ald. | 10 | A3 |
| Creechurch Pl. EC3 | Ald. | 10 | A3 |
| Creed La. EC4 | Black. | 15 | C2 |
| Crefeld Clo. W6 | Bar. Ct. | 35 | C4 |
| Crescent, The EC3 | T. Hill | 67 | C2 |
| Crescent Pl. SW3 | S. Kens. | 63 | D3 |
| Crescent Row EC1 | Barb. | 13 | C1 |
| Cresswell Gdns. SW5 | Glos. Rd. | 31 | B4 |
| Cresswell Pl. SW10 | Glos. Rd. | 31 | B4 |
| Cressy Ct. W6 | Ravens. Pk. | 35 | A1 |
| Crestfield St. WC1 | King's X | 39 | C3 |
| Cricketers Ct. SE11 | El. & Cas. | 26 | A4 |
| Crinan St. N1 | King's X | 39 | C1 |
| Cripplegate St. EC2 | Barb. | 13 | C2 |
| Crisp Rd. W6 | Hamm. | 35 | B3 |
| Crispin St. E1 | Ald. E. | 10 | B1 |
| Crofters Way NW1 | Morn. Cres. | 18 | D3 |
| Crogsland Rd. NW1 | Chalk Fm. | 18 | A2 |
| Cromer St. WC1 | King's X | 39 | C4 |
| Crompton St. W2 | Edgw. Rd. | 25 | A1 |
| Cromwell Ave. W6 | Ravens. Pk. | 35 | A2 |
| Cromwell Cres. SW5 | Earls Ct. | 24 | B2 |
| Cromwell Gdns. SW7 | S. Kens. | 63 | C2 |
| Cromwell Gro. W6 | Hamm. | 35 | B1 |
| Cromwell Ms. SW7 | S. Kens. | 63 | C3 |
| Cromwell Pl. SW7 | S. Kens. | 63 | C3 |
| Cromwell Rd. (W) SW5 | Earls Ct. | 24 | C2 |
| Cromwell Rd. (Cen) SW7 | Glos. Rd. | 31 | D2 |
| Cromwell Rd. (E) SW7 | S. Kens | 63 | B3 |

| | | | |
|---|---|---|---|
| Devonshire St. W1 | Reg. Pk. | 58 | A3 |
| Devonshire Ter. W2 | Padd. | 55 | A3 |
| Dewhurst Rd. W14 | Olym. | 35 | C1 |
| Diadem Ct. W1 | Tott. Ct. Rd. | 66 | B4 |
| Diana Pl. NW1 | Gt. Port. St. | 33 | C2 |
| Dickens Sq. SE1 | Boro. | 17 | B4 |
| Dingle Gdns. E14 | Can. Wf. | 19 | B2 |
| Dingley Pl. EC1 | Old St. | 53 | A2 |
| Disbrowe Rd. W6 | Bar. Ct. | 35 | D4 |
| Disney Pl. SE1 | Boro. | 17 | B2 |
| Disney St. SE1 | Boro. | 17 | B2 |
| Distaff La. EC4 | Mans. Ho. | 46 | B3 |
| Distillery Rd. W6 | Hamm. | 35 | B3 |
| Ditchburn St. E14 | Can. Wf. | 19 | D2 |
| Dock Rd. E16 | N. Green. | 51 | D1 |
| Dock St. E1 | Ald. E. | 10 | D4 |
| Dod St. E14 | Can. Wf. | 19 | B1 |
| Dodson St. SE1 | Lamb. N. | 41 | C2 |
| Dolben St. SE1 | S'wark | 64 | D2 |
| Dolphin La. E14 | Can. Wf. | 19 | C2 |
| Dolphin Sq. SW1 | Pim. | 57 | A4 |
| Dombey St. WC1 | Holb. | 37 | C1 |
| Dominion St. EC2 | Moor. | 50 | C2 |
| Doon St. SE1 | Water. | 71 | C1 |
| Dora St. E14 | Can. Wf. | 19 | A1 |
| Doric Way NW1 | Euston | 28 | C2 |
| Dorrington St. EC1 | Chan. La. | 21 | B2 |
| Dorset Bldgs. EC4 | Black. | 15 | B2 |
| Dorset Clo. NW1 | Mary. | 48 | C3 |
| Dorset Ms. SW1 | Vic. | 69 | A1 |
| Dorset Pl. SW1 | Pim. | 57 | B3 |
| Dorset Ri. EC4 | Black. | 15 | B2 |
| Dorset Sq. NW1 | Mary. | 48 | C2 |
| Dorset St. W1 | Baker St. | 11 | B4 |
| Dorville Cres. W6 | Ravens. Pk. | 35 | A1 |
| Doughty Ms. WC1 | Russ. Sq. | 59 | D2 |
| Doughty St. WC1 | Russ. Sq. | 59 | D1 |
| Douglas St. SW1 | Pim. | 57 | B2 |
| Douro Pl. W8 | High St. Kens. | 36 | C3 |
| Dove Ct. EC2 | Bank | 12 | B2 |
| Dove Ms. SW5 | Glos. Rd. | 31 | B3 |
| Dove Wk. SW1 | Sloane Sq. | 62 | C4 |
| Dover St. W1 | Green Pk. | 34 | B1 |
| Dover Yd. W1 | Green Pk. | 34 | B2 |
| Dowgate Hill EC4 | Cann. St. | 20 | C3 |
| Down Pl. W6 | Ravens. Pk. | 35 | A3 |
| Down St. W1 | Green Pk. | 34 | A3 |
| Down St. Ms. W1 | Green Pk. | 34 | A3 |
| Downing St. SW1 | Westmin. | 73 | B2 |
| Doyce St. SE1 | Boro. | 17 | A2 |
| D'Oyley St. SW1 | Sloane Sq. | 62 | C2 |

| | | | |
|---|---|---|---|
| Drake St. WC1 | Holb. | 37 | C2 |
| Drawdock Rd. SE10 | N. Green. | 51 | B2 |
| Draycott Pl. SW3 | Sloane Sq. | 62 | A3 |
| Draycott Ter. SW3 | Sloane Sq. | 62 | B3 |
| Drayson Ms. W8 | High St. Kens. | 36 | B2 |
| Drayton Gdns. SW10 | Glos. Rd. | 31 | C4 |
| Dreadnought St. SE10 | N. Green. | 51 | C4 |
| Drive, The, Wem. | Wem Pk. | 72 | D1 |
| Druid St. SE1 | London Br. | 45 | D4 |
| Drum St. E1 | Ald. E. | 10 | C2 |
| Drummond Cres. NW1 | Euston | 28 | C2 |
| Drummond Gate SW1 | Pim. | 57 | C3 |
| Drummond St. NW1 | Warr. St. | 70 | B2 |
| Drury Ind. Est. NW10 | Wem Pk. | 72 | D4 |
| Drury La. WC2 | Holb. | 37 | B3 |
| Dryden St. WC2 | Cov. Gdn. | 23 | C2 |
| Duchess Ms. W1 | Ox. Circ. | 54 | B1 |
| Duchess of Bedford's Wk. W8 | High St. Kens. | 36 | B2 |
| Duchess St. W1 | Ox. Circ. | 54 | B1 |
| Duchy St. SE1 | S'wark | 64 | B1 |
| Duck La. W1 | Tott. Ct. Rd. | 66 | B4 |
| Dudley St. W2 | Padd. | 55 | B1 |
| Duff St. E14 | Can. Wf. | 19 | C1 |
| Dufferin Ave. EC1 | Moor. | 50 | B1 |
| Dufferin St. EC1 | Barb. | 13 | D1 |
| Dufour's Pl. W1 | Ox. Circ. | 54 | D3 |
| Duke Hill Rd. SE1 | S'wark | 64 | C1 |
| Duke of Wellington Pl. SW1 | Hyde Pk. Cor. | 38 | C2 |
| Duke of York St. SW1 | Picc. Circ. | 56 | B3 |
| Duke St. SW1 | Picc. Circ. | 56 | B3 |
| Duke St. W1 | Bond St. | 16 | B1 |
| Duke St. Hill SE1 | London Br. | 45 | B2 |
| Dukes La. W8 | High St. Kens. | 36 | C2 |
| Duke's Ms. W1 | Bond St. | 16 | B1 |
| Dukes Pl. EC3 | Ald. | 10 | A3 |
| Duke's Rd. WC1 | Euston | 28 | D3 |
| Duke's Yd. W1 | Bond St. | 16 | B3 |
| Dulford St. W11 | Lad. Gr. | 52 | A2 |
| Duncannon St. WC2 | Char. X | 22 | B2 |
| Dunns Pas. WC1 | Holb. | 37 | B3 |
| Dunraven St. W1 | M. Arch | 47 | C3 |
| Dunsany Rd. W14 | Olym. | 35 | C1 |
| Dunstable Ms. W1 | Reg. Pk. | 58 | A3 |
| Dunster Ct. EC3 | Mon. | 49 | C2 |
| Dunsterville Way SE1 | Boro. | 17 | D3 |
| Duplex Ride SW1 | Knights. | 40 | C2 |
| Durham Ho. St. WC2 | Char. X | 22 | C2 |
| Durham St. SE11 | Vaux. | 68 | D2 |

| | | | |
|---|---|---|---|
| Durham Ter. W2 | Nott. Hill Gate | 52 | D1 |
| Durweston Ms. W1 | Baker St. | 11 | B3 |
| Durweston St. W1 | Baker St. | 11 | B4 |
| Dyer's Bldgs. EC1 | Chan. La. | 21 | B3 |
| Dyott St. WC1 | Tott. Ct. Rd. | 66 | C3 |
| Dysart St. EC2 | Old St. | 53 | D4 |

## E

| | | | |
|---|---|---|---|
| Eagle Ct. EC1 | Farr. | 30 | C2 |
| Eagle Pl. SW1 | Picc. Circ. | 56 | B2 |
| Eagle Pl. SW7 | Glos. Rd. | 31 | C4 |
| Eagle St. WC1 | Holb. | 37 | C2 |
| Eardley Cres. SW5 | Earls Ct. | 24 | B3 |
| Earl St. EC2 | Moor. | 50 | C2 |
| Earlham St. WC2 | Tott. Ct. Rd. | 66 | C4 |
| Earls Ct. Gdns. SW5 | Earls Ct. | 24 | C2 |
| Earls Ct. Rd. SW5 | Earls Ct. | 24 | B2 |
| Earls Ct. Rd. W8 | Earls Ct. | 24 | B2 |
| Earls Ct. Sq. SW5 | Earls Ct. | 24 | C3 |
| Earls Ter. W8 | High St. Kens. | 36 | A3 |
| Earls Wk. W8 | High St. Kens. | 36 | B3 |
| Earnshaw St. WC2 | Tott. Ct. Rd. | 66 | C3 |
| Earsby St. W14 | Bar. Ct. | 35 | D2 |
| Easley's Ms. W1 | Bond St. | 16 | B1 |
| East Harding St. EC4 | Chan. La. | 21 | C4 |
| East Hill, Wem. | Wem Pk. | 72 | B1 |
| East India Dock Rd. E14 | Can. Wf. | 19 | B1 |
| East India Dock Wall Rd. E14 | N. Green. | 51 | B1 |
| East Parkside SE10 | N. Green. | 51 | D3 |
| East Pas. EC1 | Barb. | 13 | C2 |
| East Poultry Ave. EC1 | Farr. | 30 | C3 |
| East Rd. N1 | Old St. | 53 | C1 |
| East Smithfield E1 | T. Hill | 67 | D3 |
| East Tenter St. E1 | Ald. E. | 10 | C3 |
| Eastbourne Ms. W2 | Padd. | 55 | A2 |
| Eastbourne Ter. W2 | Padd. | 55 | A2 |
| Eastcastle St. W1 | Ox. Circ. | 54 | C2 |
| Eastcheap EC3 | Mon. | 49 | B2 |
| Eaton Clo. SW1 | Sloane Sq. | 62 | C3 |
| Eaton Gate SW1 | Sloane Sq. | 62 | C2 |
| Eaton La. SW1 | Vic. | 69 | B2 |
| Eaton Ms. N. SW1 | Sloane Sq. | 62 | C1 |
| Eaton Ms. S. SW1 | Vic. | 69 | A2 |
| Eaton Ms. W. SW1 | Sloane Sq. | 62 | D2 |
| Eaton Pl. SW1 | Sloane Sq. | 62 | C1 |
| Eaton Row SW1 | Vic. | 69 | A2 |
| Eaton Sq. SW1 | Sloane Sq. | 62 | D2 |
| Eaton Ter. SW1 | Sloane Sq. | 62 | C2 |
| Eaton Ter. Ms. SW1 | Sloane Sq. | 62 | C2 |

| | | | |
|---|---|---|---|
| Ebbisham Dr. SW8 | Vaux. | 68 | D4 |
| Ebenezer St. N1 | Old St. | 53 | B1 |
| Ebury Ms. SW1 | Vic. | 69 | A3 |
| Ebury Ms. E. SW1 | Vic. | 69 | A2 |
| Ebury Sq. SW1 | Sloane Sq. | 62 | D3 |
| Ebury St. SW1 | Sloane Sq. | 62 | D3 |
| Eccleston Bri. SW1 | Vic. | 69 | B3 |
| Eccleston Ms. SW1 | Sloane Sq. | 62 | D1 |
| Eccleston Pl. SW1 | Vic. | 69 | A3 |
| Eccleston Sq. SW1 | Vic. | 69 | B4 |
| Eccleston Sq. Ms. SW1 | Vic. | 69 | B4 |
| Eccleston St. SW1 | Sloane Sq. | 62 | D1 |
| Ecclestone Pl., Wem. | Wem Pk. | 72 | A4 |
| Edge St. W8 | Queens. | 14 | A4 |
| Edgware Rd.(Cen) W2 | Edgw. Rd. | 25 | A1 |
| Edgware Rd. (S) W2 | M. Arch | 47 | A1 |
| Edinburgh Gate SW1 | Knights. | 40 | B2 |
| Edis St. NW1 | Cam. Tn. | 18 | A3 |
| Edith Gro. SW10 | W. Brom. | 24 | D4 |
| Edith Rd. W14 | Bar. Ct. | 35 | D2 |
| Edith Vil. W14 | W. Kens. | 24 | A3 |
| Edmond Halley Way SE10 | N. Green. | 51 | C3 |
| Edwardes Sq. W8 | High St. Kens. | 36 | A3 |
| Edwards Ms. W1 | M. Arch | 47 | D2 |
| Egbert St. NW1 | Cam. Tn. | 18 | A3 |
| Egerton Gdns. SW3 | S. Kens. | 63 | D2 |
| Egerton Gdns. Ms. SW3 | Knights. | 40 | A4 |
| Egerton Pl. SW3 | Knights. | 40 | A4 |
| Egerton Ter. SW3 | Knights. | 40 | A4 |
| Elba Pl. SE17 | El. & Cas. | 26 | D3 |
| Eldon Rd. W8 | Glos. Rd. | 31 | A1 |
| Eldon St. EC2 | Moor. | 50 | A1 |
| Elephant & Castle SE1 | El. & Cas. | 26 | B3 |
| Elephant Rd. SE17 | El. & Cas. | 26 | C3 |
| Elgin Cres. W11 | Lad. Gr. | 52 | A2 |
| Elizabeth Bri. SW1 | Vic. | 69 | A4 |
| Elizabeth Ct. SW1 | St. Jam. Pk. | 60 | D4 |
| Elizabeth St. SW1 | Sloane Sq. | 62 | D2 |
| Ellaline Rd. W6 | Bar. Ct. | 35 | C4 |
| Ellesmere St. E14 | Can. Wf. | 19 | C1 |
| Elliott Clo., Wem. | Wem Pk. | 72 | A2 |
| Elliotts Row SE11 | El. & Cas. | 26 | A3 |
| Ellis St. SW1 | Sloane Sq. | 62 | B2 |
| Elm Ct. EC4 | Temple | 65 | C2 |
| Elm Pl. SW7 | Glos. Rd. | 31 | D4 |
| Elm St. WC1 | Chan. La. | 21 | A1 |
| Elms Ms. W2 | Lanc. Gate | 42 | B2 |

| | | | |
|---|---|---|---|
| Elmside Rd., Wem. | Wem Pk. | 72 | B2 |
| Elsham Rd. W14 | Holl. Pk. | 52 | A4 |
| Elsham Ter. W14 | Holl. Pk. | 52 | A4 |
| Elvaston Ms. SW7 | Glos. Rd. | 31 | C1 |
| Elvaston Pl. SW7 | Glos. Rd. | 31 | B1 |
| Elverton St. SW1 | Pim. | 57 | B1 |
| Ely Ct. EC1 | Chan. La. | 21 | C3 |
| Ely Pl. EC1 | Chan. La. | 21 | C3 |
| Elystan St. SW3 | S. Kens. | 63 | D4 |
| Embankment Pl. WC2 | Embk. | 27 | B3 |
| Emerald St. WC1 | Holb. | 37 | C1 |
| Emery Hill St. SW1 | St. Jam. Pk. | 60 | B4 |
| Emery St. SE1 | Lamb. N. | 41 | C3 |
| Emperor's Gate SW7 | Glos. Rd. | 31 | A1 |
| Empire Ct., Wem. | Wem Pk. | 72 | C2 |
| Empire Way, Wem. | Wem Pk. | 72 | A3 |
| Empress Pl. SW6 | Earls Ct. | 24 | B3 |
| Endell St. WC2 | Tott. Ct. Rd. | 66 | D3 |
| Endsleigh Gdns. WC1 | Euston Sq. | 29 | C3 |
| Endsleigh Pl. WC1 | Russ. Sq. | 59 | A1 |
| Endsleigh St. WC1 | Russ. Sq. | 59 | A1 |
| Enford St. W1 | Mary. | 48 | C3 |
| Engineers Way, Wem. | Wem Pk. | 72 | B3 |
| English Grds. SE1 | London Br. | 45 | C3 |
| Ennismore Gdns. SW7 | S. Kens. | 63 | D1 |
| Ennismore Gdns. Ms. SW7 | S. Kens. | 63 | D1 |
| Ennismore Ms. SW7 | S. Kens. | 63 | D1 |
| Ennismore St. SW7 | S. Kens. | 63 | D1 |
| Ensign St. E1 | Ald. E. | 10 | D4 |
| Ensor Ms. SW7 | Glos. Rd. | 31 | D4 |
| Epworth St. EC2 | Old St. | 53 | C4 |
| Erasmus St. SW1 | Pim. | 57 | C2 |
| Errol St. EC1 | Barb. | 13 | D1 |
| Essex Ct. EC4 | Temple | 65 | C1 |
| Essex St. WC2 | Temple | 65 | C2 |
| Essex Vil. W8 | High St. Kens. | 36 | B3 |
| Esterbrooke St. SW1 | Pim. | 57 | B2 |
| Ethel St. SE17 | El. & Cas. | 26 | D4 |
| Ettrick St. E14 | Can. Wf. | 19 | D1 |
| Euston Cen. NW1 | Warr. St. | 70 | B2 |
| Euston Gro. NW1 | Euston | 28 | C3 |
| Euston Rd. NW1 (N) | King's X | 39 | A4 |
| Euston Rd. (Cen) NW1 | Euston | 28 | C4 |
| Euston Rd. (Cen) NW1 | Euston Sq. | 29 | C3 |
| Euston Rd. (Cen) NW1 | Warr. St. | 70 | A3 |
| Euston Rd. (S) NW1 | Gt. Port. St. | 33 | C3 |
| Euston Sq. NW1 | Euston | 28 | C3 |

| | | | |
|---|---|---|---|
| Euston Sta. Colonnade NW1 | Euston | 28 | C3 |
| Euston St. NW1 | Euston Sq. | 29 | B2 |
| Evelyn Yd. W1 | Tott. Ct. Rd. | 66 | B3 |
| Everington St. W6 | Bar. Ct. | 35 | C4 |
| Eversholt St. NW1 | Morn. Cres. | 18 | C4 |
| Eversley Ave., Wem. | Wem Pk. | 72 | B1 |
| Everton Bldgs. NW1 | Euston Sq. | 29 | A2 |
| Ewer St. SE1 | Boro. | 17 | A1 |
| Excel Ct. WC2 | Leic. Sq. | 43 | B3 |
| Exchange Arc. EC2 | Liv. St. | 44 | C1 |
| Exchange Ct. WC2 | Char. X | 22 | C2 |
| Exchange Pl. EC2 | Liv. St. | 44 | B1 |
| Exchange Sq. EC2 | Liv. St. | 44 | B1 |
| Exeter St. WC2 | Cov. Gdn. | 23 | C3 |
| Exhibition Rd. SW7 | S. Kens. | 63 | C1 |
| Exmouth Ms. NW1 | Euston Sq. | 29 | B2 |
| Exton St. SE1 | Water. | 71 | C2 |
| Eyre St. Hill EC1 | Chan. La. | 21 | B1 |

## F

| | | | |
|---|---|---|---|
| Fair St. SE1 | London Br. | 45 | D4 |
| Fairholme Rd. W14 | Bar. Ct. | 35 | D3 |
| Fairholt St. SW7 | Knights. | 40 | A3 |
| Falcon Clo. SE1 | S'wark | 64 | D1 |
| Falconberg Ct. W1 | Tott. Ct. Rd. | 66 | C3 |
| Falconberg Ms. W1 | Tott. Ct. Rd. | 66 | B3 |
| Falmouth Rd. SE1 | El. & Cas. | 26 | D2 |
| Fann St. EC1 | Barb. | 13 | C1 |
| Fann St. EC2 | Barb. | 13 | C1 |
| Fanshaw St. N1 | Old St. | 53 | D1 |
| Fareham St. W1 | Tott. Ct. Rd. | 66 | B3 |
| Farm La. SW6 | W. Brom. | 24 | B4 |
| Farm St. W1 | Bond St. | 16 | C4 |
| Farnham Pl. SE1 | S'wark | 64 | D2 |
| Faroe Rd. W14 | Olym. | 35 | C1 |
| Farrance St. E14 | Can. Wf. | 19 | B1 |
| Farrier St. NW1 | Cam. Tn. | 18 | B2 |
| Farrier Wk. SW10 | W. Brom. | 24 | D4 |
| Farringdon La. EC1 | Farr. | 30 | B1 |
| Farringdon Rd. EC4 | Black. | 15 | B1 |
| Fashion St. E1 | Ald. E. | 10 | C1 |
| Faulkner's All. EC1 | Farr. | 30 | C2 |
| Fawcett St. SW10 | W. Brom. | 24 | C4 |
| Featherstone St. EC1 | Old St. | 53 | B3 |
| Felgate Ms. W6 | Ravens. Pk. | 35 | A2 |
| Fen Ct. EC3 | Mon. | 49 | C2 |
| Fenchurch Ave. EC3 | Mon. | 49 | C1 |
| Fenchurch Bldgs. EC3 | Ald. | 10 | A3 |
| Fenchurch Pl. EC3 | T. Hill | 67 | B2 |
| Fenchurch St. EC3 | Mon. | 49 | C2 |

| | | | |
|---|---|---|---|
| Fenelon Pl. W14 | W. Kens. | 24 | A2 |
| Fenning St. SE1 | London Br. | 45 | C4 |
| Fentiman Rd. SW8 | Vaux. | 68 | D4 |
| Ferdinand St. NW1 | Chalk Fm. | 18 | A2 |
| Fernshaw Rd. SW10 | W. Brom. | 24 | D4 |
| Fetter La. EC4 | Black. | 15 | A2 |
| Field Ct. WC1 | Chan. La. | 21 | A3 |
| Field Rd. W6 | Bar. Ct. | 35 | D3 |
| Field St. WC1 | King's X | 39 | D3 |
| Fielding Rd. W14 | Olym. | 35 | C1 |
| Fifth Way, Wem. | Wem Pk. | 72 | C3 |
| Finborough Rd. SW10 | Earls Ct. | 24 | C3 |
| Finch La. EC3 | Bank | 12 | C2 |
| Finck St. SE1 | Lamb. N. | 41 | B2 |
| Findhorn St. E14 | Can. Wf. | 19 | D1 |
| Finsbury Ave. EC2 | Moor. | 50 | C3 |
| Finsbury Circ. EC2 | Moor. | 50 | C3 |
| Finsbury Mkt. EC2 | Old St. | 53 | D4 |
| Finsbury Pavement EC2 | Moor. | 50 | C2 |
| Finsbury Sq. EC2 | Old St. | 53 | C4 |
| Finsbury St. EC2 | Moor. | 50 | B2 |
| First Way, Wem. | Wem Pk. | 72 | C3 |
| Fish St. Hill EC3 | Mon. | 49 | B3 |
| Fisher St. WC1 | Holb. | 37 | C2 |
| Fitzgeorge Ave. W14 | Bar. Ct. | 35 | D2 |
| Fitzhardinge St. W1 | M. Arch | 47 | D1 |
| Fitzjames Ave. W14 | Bar. Ct. | 35 | D2 |
| Fitzmaurice Pl. W1 | Green Pk. | 34 | B2 |
| Fitzroy Ct. W1 | Warr. St. | 70 | C3 |
| Fitzroy Ms. W1 | Warr. St. | 70 | B3 |
| Fitzroy Rd. NW1 | Cam. Tn. | 18 | A3 |
| Fitzroy Sq. W1 | Warr. St. | 70 | B3 |
| Fitzroy St. W1 | Warr. St. | 70 | B3 |
| Flank St. E1 | Ald. E. | 10 | D4 |
| Flaxman Ct. W1 | Tott. Ct. Rd. | 66 | B4 |
| Flaxman Ter. WC1 | Euston | 28 | D3 |
| Fleet St. EC4 | Black. | 15 | A2 |
| Fleming Ct. W2 | Edgw. Rd. | 25 | A2 |
| Flitcroft St. WC2 | Tott. Ct. Rd. | 66 | C4 |
| Flora Clo. E14 | Can. Wf. | 19 | C1 |
| Floral St. WC2 | Leic. Sq. | 43 | C2 |
| Flower & Dean Wk. E1 | Ald. E. | 10 | C1 |
| Flower Wk., The SW7 | High St. Kens. | 36 | D2 |
| Foley St. W1 | Goodge St. | 32 | A3 |
| Folgate St. E1 | Liv. St. | 44 | C1 |
| Follett St. E14 | Can. Wf. | 19 | D1 |
| Folly Wall E14 | Can. Wf. | 19 | D4 |
| Fore St. EC2 | Moor. | 50 | A3 |
| Fore St. Ave. EC2 | Moor. | 50 | B3 |

| | | | |
|---|---|---|---|
| Forset St. W1 | Edgw. Rd. | 25 | D4 |
| Fort St. E1 | Liv. St. | 44 | C2 |
| Fortune St. EC1 | Barb. | 13 | D1 |
| Forty Ave., Wem. | Wem Pk. | 72 | A2 |
| Forty Clo., Wem. | Wem Pk. | 72 | A2 |
| Forty La., Wem. | Wem Pk. | 72 | C1 |
| Fosbury Ms. W2 | Queens. | 14 | C3 |
| Foster La. EC2 | St. Paul's | 61 | C2 |
| Foubert's Pl. W1 | Ox. Circ. | 54 | C3 |
| Founders Ct. EC2 | Bank | 12 | B1 |
| Foundry Ms. NW1 | Euston Sq. | 29 | B3 |
| Fountain Ct. EC4 | Temple | 65 | C2 |
| Fountain Sq. SW1 | Vic. | 69 | A3 |
| Fourth Way, Wem. | Wem Pk. | 72 | D3 |
| Fox and Knot St. EC1 | Barb. | 13 | B2 |
| Frampton St. NW8 | Edgw. Rd. | 25 | B1 |
| Francis St. SW1 | Vic. | 69 | C3 |
| Frankland Rd. SW7 | S. Kens. | 63 | B3 |
| Franklin's Row SW3 | Sloane Sq. | 62 | B4 |
| Frazier St. SE1 | Lamb. N. | 41 | B2 |
| Frederic Ms. SW1 | Knights. | 40 | C2 |
| Frederick Clo. W2 | M. Arch | 47 | A3 |
| Frederick St. WC1 | King's X | 39 | D4 |
| Frederick's Pl. EC2 | Bank | 12 | B2 |
| Friar St. EC4 | Black. | 15 | C2 |
| Friars Mead E14 | N. Green. | 51 | A4 |
| Friary Ct. SW1 | Green Pk. | 34 | D3 |
| Friday St. EC4 | St. Paul's | 61 | C3 |
| Frith St. W1 | Tott. Ct. Rd. | 66 | B4 |
| Frostic Wk. E1 | Ald. E. | 10 | D1 |
| Frying Pan All. E1 | Ald. E. | 10 | B1 |
| Fulham Palace Rd. SW6 | Bar. Ct. | 35 | C4 |
| Fulham Palace Rd. W6 | Hamm. | 35 | B3 |
| Fullwoods Ms. N1 | Old St. | 53 | C1 |
| Fulton Ms. W2 | Bays. | 14 | D2 |
| Fulton Rd., Wem. | Wem Pk. | 72 | B2 |
| Fulwood Pl. WC1 | Chan. La. | 21 | A3 |
| Furber St. W6 | Ravens. Pk. | 35 | A1 |
| Furnival St. EC4 | Chan. La. | 21 | B4 |
| Fynes St. SW1 | Pim. | 57 | B1 |

## G

| | | | |
|---|---|---|---|
| Gables, The, Wem. | Wem Pk. | 72 | A3 |
| Gabrielle Clo., Wem. | Wem Pk. | 72 | A2 |
| Gage St. WC1 | Russ. Sq. | 59 | C3 |
| Gaisford St. NW5 | Cam. Tn. | 18 | C1 |
| Galbraith St. E14 | N. Green. | 51 | A4 |
| Galen Pl. WC1 | Holb. | 37 | C2 |
| Galena Rd. W6 | Ravens. Pk. | 35 | A2 |

| | | | | | | | | |
|---|---|---|---|---|---|---|---|
| Galway St. EC1 | Old St. | 53 | A2 | Gilston Rd. SW10 | Earls Ct. | 24 | D3 |
| Gambia St. SE1 | S'wark | 64 | D2 | Giltspur St. EC1 | St. Paul's | 61 | B2 |
| Ganton St. W1 | Ox. Circ. | 54 | C4 | Giraud St. E14 | Can. Wf. | 19 | C1 |
| Garbutt Pl. W1 | Reg. Pk. | 58 | A3 | Girdlers Rd. W14 | Hamm. | 35 | C2 |
| Garden Ct. EC4 | Temple | 65 | C2 | Gladstone St. SE1 | Lamb. N. | 41 | D3 |
| Garden Ms. W2 | Queens. | 14 | A3 | Glasshill St. SE1 | S'wark | 64 | D3 |
| Garden Row SE1 | El. & Cas. | 26 | A2 | Glasshouse All. EC4 | Black. | 15 | A2 |
| Garden Ter. SW1 | Pim. | 57 | B3 | Glasshouse St. W1 | Picc. Circ. | 56 | B2 |
| Garden Wk. EC2 | Old St. | 53 | D2 | Glasshouse Wk. SE11 | Vaux. | 68 | C1 |
| Gardners La. EC4 | Mans. Ho. | 46 | B3 | Glasshouse Yd. EC1 | Barb. | 13 | C1 |
| Garford St. E14 | Can. Wf. | 19 | B2 | Glazbury Rd. W14 | Bar. Ct. | 35 | D2 |
| Garlick Hill EC4 | Mans. Ho. | 46 | C3 | Gledhow Gdns. SW5 | Glos. Rd. | 31 | B3 |
| Garrett St. EC1 | Old St. | 53 | A3 | Gledstanes Rd. W14 | Bar. Ct. | 35 | D3 |
| Garrick St. WC2 | Leic. Sq. | 43 | C2 | Glendower Pl. SW7 | S. Kens. | 63 | B3 |
| Garway Rd. W2 | Bays. | 14 | B1 | Glengall Gro. E14 | N. Green. | 51 | A4 |
| Gaselee St. E14 | Can. Wf. | 19 | D2 | Glenthorne Rd. W6 | Ravens. Pk. | 35 | A2 |
| Gaspar Clo. SW5 | Glos. Rd. | 31 | A2 | Glentworth St. NW1 | Baker St. | 11 | B2 |
| Gaspar Ms. SW5 | Glos. Rd. | 31 | A2 | Gliddon Rd. W14 | Bar. Ct. | 35 | D2 |
| Gastein Rd. W6 | Bar. Ct. | 35 | C4 | Globe St. SE1 | Boro. | 17 | C3 |
| Gate Ms. SW7 | Knights. | 40 | A2 | Globe Yd. W1 | Bond St. | 16 | C2 |
| Gate St. WC2 | Holb. | 37 | C3 | Gloucester Ave. NW1 | Chalk Fm. | 18 | A2 |
| Gateforth St. NW8 | Edgw. Rd. | 25 | C1 | Gloucester Ct. EC3 | T. Hill | 67 | B3 |
| Gatesborough St. EC2 | Old St. | 53 | D3 | Gloucester Cres. NW1 | Cam. Tn. | 18 | B3 |
| Gaunt St. SE1 | El. & Cas. | 26 | B1 | Gloucester Gate NW1 | Morn. Cres. | 18 | B4 |
| Gaywood Est. SE1 | El. & Cas. | 26 | B2 | Gloucester Ms. W2 | Padd. | 55 | A3 |
| Gaywood St. SE1 | El. & Cas. | 26 | B2 | Gloucester Ms. W. W2 | Bays. | 14 | D1 |
| Gees Ct. W1 | Bond St. | 16 | B2 | Gloucester Pl. NW1 | Mary. | 48 | C1 |
| George Ct. WC2 | Char. X | 22 | C2 | Gloucester Pl. W1 | Baker St. | 11 | B3 |
| George Inn Yd. SE1 | London Br. | 45 | A3 | Gloucester Pl. Ms. W1 | Baker St. | 11 | B4 |
| George Ms. NW1 | Euston | 29 | A2 | Gloucester Rd. SW7 | High St. Kens. | 36 | D3 |
| George St. W1 | M. Arch | 47 | B1 | Gloucester Sq. W2 | Padd. | 55 | C3 |
| George Yd. EC3 | Bank | 12 | C2 | Gloucester Ter. W2 | Nott. Hill Gate | 52 | D1 |
| George Yd. W1 | Bond St. | 16 | B3 | Gloucester Wk. W8 | High St. Kens. | 36 | D2 |
| Georgiana St. NW1 | Cam. Tn. | 18 | C3 | Glyn St. SE11 | Vaux. | 68 | D2 |
| Gerald Ms. SW1 | Sloane Sq. | 62 | D2 | Glynde Ms. SW3 | Knights. | 40 | A4 |
| Gerald Rd. SW1 | Sloane Sq. | 62 | D2 | Goding St. SE11 | Vaux. | 68 | C2 |
| Geraldine St. SE11 | El. & Cas. | 26 | A2 | Godliman St. EC4 | St. Paul's | 61 | C3 |
| Gerrard Pl. W1 | Leic. Sq. | 43 | B2 | Golden La. EC1 | Barb. | 13 | C1 |
| Gerrard St. W1 | Leic. Sq. | 43 | B2 | Golden La. Est. EC1 | Barb. | 13 | C1 |
| Gerridge St. SE1 | Lamb. N. | 41 | C3 | Golden Sq. W1 | Picc. Circ. | 56 | B1 |
| Gertrude St. SW10 | W. Brom. | 24 | D4 | Goldington Cres. NW1 | Morn. Cres. | 18 | D4 |
| Gervase Clo., Wem. | Wem Pk. | 72 | D2 | Goldington Cres. | Morn. Cres. | 18 | D4 |
| Gibbs Grn. W14 | W. Kens. | 24 | A3 | Gdns. NW1 | | | |
| Gilbert Pl. WC1 | Tott. Ct. Rd. | 66 | D2 | Goldington St. NW1 | Morn. Cres. | 18 | D4 |
| Gilbert St. W1 | Bond St. | 16 | B2 | Goldsmith St. EC2 | St. Paul's | 61 | D2 |
| Gildea St. W1 | Ox. Circ. | 54 | B1 | Goodge Pl. W1 | Goodge St. | 32 | B3 |
| Gill St. E14 | Can. Wf. | 19 | A2 | Goodge St. W1 | Goodge St. | 32 | B3 |
| Gillfoot NW1 | Euston | 28 | A1 | Goodman's Flds. E1 | Ald. E. | 10 | D3 |
| Gillingham Ms. SW1 | Vic. | 69 | C3 | Goodman's Stile E1 | Ald. E. | 10 | D2 |
| Gillingham Row SW1 | Vic. | 69 | C3 | Goodmans Yd. E1 | T. Hill | 67 | C2 |
| Gillingham St. SW1 | Vic. | 69 | B3 | Goods Way NW1 | King's X | 39 | B1 |

| | | | |
|---|---|---|---|
| Hamilton Sq. SE1 | London Br. | 45 | B4 |
| Hamlet Way SE1 | London Br. | 45 | B4 |
| Hammersmith Bri. SW13 | Ravens. Pk. | 35 | A3 |
| Hammersmith Bri. Rd. W6 | Hamm. | 35 | B3 |
| Hammersmith Bdy. W6 | Hamm. | 35 | B2 |
| Hammersmith Flyover W6 | Hamm. | 35 | B3 |
| Hammersmith Rd. W6 | Hamm. | 35 | C2 |
| Hammersmith Rd. W14 | Hamm. | 35 | C2 |
| Hammett St. EC3 | T. Hill | 67 | C2 |
| Hammond St. NW5 | Cam. Tn. | 18 | C1 |
| Hampden Clo. NW1 | King's X | 39 | A2 |
| Hampden Gurney St. W1 | M. Arch | 47 | B2 |
| Hampstead Rd. NW1 | Euston | 28 | A1 |
| Hampton St. SE1 | El. & Cas. | 26 | B4 |
| Hampton St. SE17 | El. & Cas. | 26 | B4 |
| Hand Ct. WC1 | Chan. La. | 21 | A3 |
| Handel St. WC1 | Russ. Sq. | 59 | B1 |
| Hankey Pl. SE1 | Boro. | 17 | D3 |
| Hannah Clo. NW10 | Wem Pk. | 72 | D3 |
| Hanover Pl. WC2 | Cov. Gdn. | 23 | C2 |
| Hanover Sq. W1 | Ox. Circ. | 54 | B3 |
| Hanover St. W1 | Ox. Circ. | 54 | B3 |
| Hans Cres. SW1 | Knights. | 40 | C2 |
| Hans Pl. SW1 | Knights. | 40 | C3 |
| Hans Rd. SW3 | Knights. | 40 | B3 |
| Hans St. SW1 | Knights. | 40 | C4 |
| Hanson St. W1 | Goodge St. | 32 | A2 |
| Hanway Pl. W1 | Tott. Ct. Rd. | 66 | B3 |
| Hanway St. W1 | Tott. Ct. Rd. | 66 | B3 |
| Harbet Rd. W2 | Edgw. Rd. | 25 | B3 |
| Harbour Ex. Sq. E14 | Can. Wf. | 19 | C4 |
| Harcourt St. W1 | Edgw. Rd. | 25 | D3 |
| Harcourt Ter. SW10 | Earls Ct. | 24 | C3 |
| Hardwidge St. SE1 | London Br. | 45 | C4 |
| Hare Ct. EC4 | Temple | 65 | C1 |
| Hare Pl. EC4 | Black. | 15 | A2 |
| Harewood Ave. NW1 | Mary. | 48 | B2 |
| Harewood Pl. W1 | Ox. Circ. | 54 | B3 |
| Harewood Row NW1 | Mary. | 48 | B2 |
| Harley Gdns. SW10 | Earls Ct. | 24 | D3 |
| Harley Pl. W1 | Reg. Pk. | 58 | B4 |
| Harley St. W1 | Reg. Pk. | 58 | B2 |
| Harleyford Rd. SE11 | Vaux. | 68 | D3 |
| Harmood St. NW1 | Chalk Fm. | 18 | B1 |
| Harp All. EC4 | Black. | 15 | B1 |
| Harp La. EC3 | Mon. | 49 | C3 |
| Harper Rd. SE1 | Boro. | 17 | B4 |
| Harpur Ms. WC1 | Holb. | 37 | C1 |
| Harpur St. WC1 | Holb. | 37 | C1 |
| Harrap St. E14 | Can. Wf. | 19 | D2 |
| Harriet St. SW1 | Knights. | 40 | C2 |
| Harriet Wk. SW1 | Knights. | 40 | C2 |
| Harrington Gdns. SW7 | Glos. Rd. | 31 | A3 |
| Harrington Rd. SW7 | S. Kens. | 63 | C1 |
| Harrington Sq. NW1 | Euston | 28 | A1 |
| Harrington St. NW1 | Euston | 28 | A1 |
| Harrison St. WC1 | King's X | 39 | C4 |
| Harrow La. E14 | Can. Wf. | 19 | D2 |
| Harrow Pl. E1 | Ald. | 10 | A2 |
| Harrow Rd. (Tokyngton), Wem. | Wem Pk. | 72 | B4 |
| Harrowby St. W1 | Edgw. Rd. | 25 | D4 |
| Hart St. EC3 | T. Hill | 67 | B2 |
| Hartland Rd. NW1 | Cam. Tn. | 18 | B2 |
| Hartshorn All. EC3 | Ald. | 10 | A3 |
| Harwich La. EC2 | Liv. St. | 44 | C1 |
| Hastings St. WC1 | King's X | 39 | B4 |
| Hat and Mitre Ct. EC1 | Barb. | 13 | B1 |
| Hatfields SE1 | S'wark | 64 | B1 |
| Hatherley Gro. W2 | Nott. Hill Gate | 52 | B1 |
| Hatherley St. SW1 | Pim. | 57 | A2 |
| Hatton Gdn. EC1 | Farr. | 30 | B2 |
| Hatton Pl. EC1 | Farr. | 30 | B2 |
| Hatton Row NW8 | Edgw. Rd. | 25 | B1 |
| Hatton St. NW8 | Edgw. Rd. | 25 | B1 |
| Hatton Wall EC1 | Chan. La. | 21 | B2 |
| Haunch of Venison Yd. W1 | Bond St. | 16 | C2 |
| Havannah St. E14 | Can. Wf. | 19 | B4 |
| Havenwood, Wem. | Wem Pk. | 72 | C2 |
| Hawksmoor St. W6 | Bar. Ct. | 35 | C4 |
| Hawley Cres. NW1 | Cam. Tn. | 18 | B2 |
| Hawley Rd. NW1 | Cam. Tn. | 18 | B2 |
| Hawley St. NW1 | Cam. Tn. | 18 | B2 |
| Hay Currie St. E14 | Can. Wf. | 19 | C1 |
| Hay Hill W1 | Green Pk. | 34 | B1 |
| Haydon St. EC3 | T. Hill | 67 | C2 |
| Haydon Wk. E1 | T. Hill | 67 | D2 |
| Hayes Pl. NW1 | Mary. | 48 | B2 |
| Hayles St. SE11 | El. & Cas. | 26 | A3 |
| Haymarket SW1 | Picc. Circ. | 56 | C2 |
| Haymarket Arc. SW1 | Picc. Circ. | 56 | C2 |
| Hayne St. EC1 | Barb. | 13 | B2 |
| Hay's La. SE1 | London Br. | 45 | C3 |
| Hay's Ms. W1 | Green Pk. | 34 | A2 |

| | | | |
|---|---|---|---|
| Hayward's Pl. EC1 | Farr. | 30 | C1 |
| Hazlitt Rd. W14 | Olym. | 35 | D1 |
| Headfort Pl. SW1 | Hyde Pk. Cor. | 38 | C3 |
| Healey St. NW1 | Chalk Fm. | 18 | B1 |
| Heathcote St. WC1 | Russ. Sq. | 59 | D1 |
| Hebron Rd. W6 | Ravens. Pk. | 35 | A1 |
| Heddon St. W1 | Ox. Circ. | 54 | C4 |
| Helmet Row EC1 | Old St. | 53 | A3 |
| Heneage La. EC3 | Ald. | 10 | A3 |
| Henrietta Ms. WC1 | Russ. Sq. | 59 | C1 |
| Henrietta Pl. W1 | Bond St. | 16 | C1 |
| Henrietta St. WC2 | Cov. Gdn. | 23 | C3 |
| Herald's Ct. SE11 | El. & Cas. | 26 | A4 |
| Herbal Hill EC1 | Farr. | 30 | B1 |
| Herbert Cres. SW1 | Knights. | 40 | C3 |
| Herbert St. NW5 | Chalk Fm. | 18 | A1 |
| Herbrand St. WC1 | Russ. Sq. | 59 | B1 |
| Hercules Rd. SE1 | Lamb. N. | 41 | A4 |
| Hereford Ms. W2 | Bays. | 14 | A1 |
| Hereford Rd. W2 | Nott. Hill Gate | 52 | C1 |
| Hereford Sq. SW7 | Glos. Rd. | 31 | C3 |
| Hermitage St. W2 | Padd. | 55 | B1 |
| Heron Quay E14 | Can. Wf. | 19 | B3 |
| Herrick St. SW1 | Pim. | 57 | C2 |
| Hertford Pl. W1 | Warr. St. | 70 | B3 |
| Hertford St. W1 | Hyde Pk. Cor. | 38 | C1 |
| Hertsmere Rd. E14 | Can. Wf. | 19 | B2 |
| Hesketh Pl. W11 | Lad. Gr. | 52 | A2 |
| Hesper Ms. SW5 | Earls Ct. | 24 | C3 |
| Heygate St. SE17 | El. & Cas. | 26 | C4 |
| Hide Pl. SW1 | Pim. | 57 | B2 |
| High Holborn (W) WC1 | Tott. Ct. Rd. | 66 | D3 |
| High Holborn (Cen) WC1 | Holb. | 37 | A3 |
| High Holborn (E) WC1 | Chan. La. | 21 | A3 |
| High St., Wem. | Wem Pk. | 72 | A3 |
| High Timber St. EC4 | Mans. Ho. | 46 | B3 |
| Hildyard Rd. SW6 | W. Brom. | 24 | B4 |
| Hillcroft Cres., Wem. | Wem Pk. | 72 | A3 |
| Hillgate Pl. W8 | Nott. Hill Gate | 52 | C3 |
| Hillgate St. W8 | Nott. Hill Gate | 52 | C3 |
| Hills Pl. W1 | Ox. Circ. | 54 | C3 |
| Hillside Ave., Wem. | Wem Pk. | 72 | A3 |
| Hillsleigh Rd. W8 | Holl. Pk. | 52 | B3 |
| Hind Ct. EC4 | Black. | 15 | A2 |
| Hind Gro. E14 | Can. Wf. | 19 | B1 |
| Hinde St. W1 | Bond St. | 16 | B1 |
| Hippodrome Pl. W11 | Lad. Gr. | 52 | A2 |
| Hobart Pl. SW1 | Vic. | 69 | A1 |
| Hobury St. SW10 | W. Brom. | 24 | D4 |

| | | | |
|---|---|---|---|
| Hofland Rd. W14 | Olym. | 35 | C1 |
| Hogan Ms. W2 | Edgw. Rd. | 25 | A2 |
| Hogarth Ct. EC3 | T. Hill | 67 | B2 |
| Hogarth Rd. SW5 | Earls Ct. | 24 | C2 |
| Holbein Ms. SW1 | Sloane Sq. | 62 | C4 |
| Holbein Pl. SW1 | Sloane Sq. | 62 | C4 |
| Holborn EC1 | Chan. La. | 21 | B3 |
| Holborn Circ. EC1 | Chan. La. | 21 | C3 |
| Holborn Pl. WC1 | Holb. | 37 | C2 |
| Holborn Viaduct EC1 | Chan. La. | 21 | C3 |
| Holcombe St. W6 | Ravens. Pk. | 35 | A3 |
| Holland Gdns. W14 | Olym. | 35 | D1 |
| Holland Pk. W8 | Holl. Pk. | 52 | B4 |
| Holland Pk. W11 | Holl. Pk. | 52 | A3 |
| Holland Pk. Ave. W11 | Holl. Pk. | 52 | A3 |
| Holland Pk. Gdns. W14 | Holl. Pk. | 52 | A4 |
| Holland Pk. Ms. W11 | Holl. Pk. | 52 | B3 |
| Holland Pk. Rd. W14 | High St. Kens. | 36 | A3 |
| Holland St. SE1 | S'wark | 64 | D1 |
| Holland St. W8 | High St. Kens. | 36 | B2 |
| Holland Vil. Rd. W14 | Holl. Pk. | 52 | A4 |
| Holland Wk. W8 | Holl. Pk. | 52 | B4 |
| Hollen St. W1 | Ox. Circ. | 54 | D2 |
| Holles St. W1 | Ox. Circ. | 54 | B2 |
| Hollycroft Ave., Wem. | Wem Pk. | 72 | A1 |
| Hollywood Rd. SW10 | W. Brom. | 24 | D4 |
| Holmes Rd. NW5 | Chalk Fm. | 18 | B1 |
| Holmes Ter. SE1 | Water. | 71 | C3 |
| Holsworthy Sq. WC1 | Chan. La. | 21 | A1 |
| Holyoak Rd. SE11 | El. & Cas. | 26 | A3 |
| Holyrood St. SE1 | London Br. | 45 | C3 |
| Holywell Row EC2 | Old St. | 53 | D4 |
| Homer Row W1 | Edgw. Rd. | 25 | D3 |
| Homer St. W1 | Edgw. Rd. | 25 | D3 |
| Honey La. EC2 | Mans. Ho. | 46 | C2 |
| Hood Ct. EC4 | Black. | 15 | A2 |
| Hooper St. E1 | Ald. E. | 10 | D3 |
| Hooper's Ct. SW3 | Knights. | 40 | B2 |
| Hopetown St. E1 | Ald. E. | 10 | C1 |
| Hopkins St. W1 | Ox. Circ. | 54 | D3 |
| Hopton Gdns. SE1 | S'wark | 64 | D1 |
| Hopton St. SE1 | S'wark | 64 | D1 |
| Horbury Cres. W11 | Nott. Hill Gate | 52 | C2 |
| Hornton St. W8 | High St. Kens. | 36 | B2 |
| Horse and Dolphin Yd. W1 | Leic. Sq. | 43 | B2 |
| Horse Guards Ave. SW1 | Char. X | 22 | B4 |

| | | | |
|---|---|---|---|
| Horse Guards Rd. SW1 | Char. X | 22 | A4 |
| Horse Ride SW1 | Picc. Circ. | 56 | C4 |
| Horse Shoe Yd. W1 | Ox. Circ. | 54 | B4 |
| Horseferry Rd. SW1 | St. Jam. Pk. | 60 | C4 |
| Hosier La. EC1 | Farr. | 30 | C3 |
| Houghton St. WC2 | Temple | 65 | B1 |
| Houndsditch EC3 | Ald. | 10 | A2 |
| Howard Pl. SW1 | Vic. | 69 | C2 |
| Howell Wk. SE1 | El. & Cas. | 26 | B4 |
| Howick Pl. SW1 | St. Jam. Pk. | 60 | B4 |
| Howland Ms. E. W1 | Goodge St. | 32 | B2 |
| Howland St. W1 | Goodge St. | 32 | A2 |
| Hoxton Mkt. N1 | Old St. | 53 | D2 |
| Hoxton Sq. N1 | Old St. | 53 | D2 |
| Hudson's Pl. SW1 | Vic. | 69 | C3 |
| Huggin Ct. EC4 | Mans. Ho. | 46 | C3 |
| Huggin Hill EC4 | Mans. Ho. | 46 | C3 |
| Hugh Ms. SW1 | Vic. | 69 | B4 |
| Hugh Pl. SW1 | Pim. | 57 | B1 |
| Hugh St. SW1 | Vic. | 69 | B4 |
| Humbolt Rd. W6 | Bar. Ct. | 35 | D4 |
| Hungerford Bri. SE1 | Water. | 71 | A2 |
| Hungerford Bri. WC2 | Embk. | 27 | C4 |
| Hungerford La. WC2 | Embk. | 27 | B3 |
| Hungerford Rd. N7 | Cam. Tn. | 18 | D1 |
| Hunter St. WC1 | Russ. Sq. | 59 | C1 |
| Huntley St. WC1 | Warr. St. | 70 | C3 |
| Hunt's Ct. WC2 | Leic. Sq. | 43 | B3 |
| Huntsworth Ms. NW1 | Mary. | 48 | C2 |
| Hutchings St. E14 | Can. Wf. | 19 | B4 |
| Hutton St. EC4 | Black. | 15 | A2 |
| Hyde Pk. SW7 | Lanc. Gate | 42 | D4 |
| Hyde Pk. W1 | Lanc. Gate | 42 | D4 |
| Hyde Pk. W2 | Lanc. Gate | 42 | D4 |
| Hyde Pk. Cor. W1 | Hyde Pk. Cor. | 38 | C2 |
| Hyde Pk. Cres. W2 | Padd. | 55 | D3 |
| Hyde Pk. Gdns. W2 | Lanc. Gate | 42 | C2 |
| Hyde Pk. Gdns. Ms. W2 | Lanc. Gate | 42 | C2 |
| Hyde Pk. Gate SW7 | High St. Kens. | 36 | D2 |
| Hyde Pk. Pl. W2 | M. Arch | 47 | A3 |
| Hyde Pk. Sq. W2 | Padd. | 55 | D3 |
| Hyde Pk. Sq. Ms. W2 | Padd. | 55 | D3 |
| Hyde Pk. St. W2 | Padd. | 55 | D3 |

## I

| | | | |
|---|---|---|---|
| Ida St. E14 | Can. Wf. | 19 | D1 |
| Idol La. EC3 | Mon. | 49 | C3 |
| Iffley Rd. W6 | Ravens. Pk. | 35 | A1 |

| | | | |
|---|---|---|---|
| Ifield Rd. SW10 | W. Brom. | 24 | C4 |
| Ilchester Gdns. W2 | Bays. | 14 | B2 |
| Ilchester Pl. W14 | High St. Kens. | 36 | A3 |
| Imperial College Rd. SW7 | S. Kens. | 63 | B1 |
| Indescon Ct. E14 | Can. Wf. | 19 | B4 |
| India Pl. WC2 | Temple | 65 | A2 |
| India St. EC3 | Ald. | 10 | B3 |
| Ingestre Pl. W1 | Ox. Circ. | 54 | D3 |
| Inigo Pl. WC2 | Leic. Sq. | 43 | C2 |
| Inkerman Rd. NW5 | Chalk Fm. | 18 | B1 |
| Inner Temple La. EC4 | Temple | 65 | C1 |
| Inver Ct. W2 | Bays. | 14 | C1 |
| Inverness Ms. W2 | Bays. | 14 | C2 |
| Inverness Pl. W2 | Bays. | 14 | C2 |
| Inverness St. NW1 | Cam. Tn. | 18 | B3 |
| Inverness Ter. W2 | Bays. | 14 | C2 |
| Ireland Yd. EC4 | Black. | 15 | C2 |
| Ironmonger La. EC2 | Bank | 12 | B2 |
| Ironmonger Pas. EC1 | Old St. | 53 | A2 |
| Ironmonger Row EC1 | Old St. | 53 | A2 |
| Irving Rd. W14 | Olym. | 35 | C1 |
| Irving St. WC2 | Leic. Sq. | 43 | B3 |
| Isabella St. SE1 | S'wark | 64 | C2 |
| Isambard Ms. E14 | N. Green. | 51 | A4 |
| Ivatt Pl. W14 | W. Kens. | 24 | A3 |
| Iverna Ct. W8 | High St. Kens. | 36 | B3 |
| Iverna Gdns. W8 | High St. Kens. | 36 | B3 |
| Ivor Pl. NW1 | Mary. | 48 | C2 |
| Ivor St. NW1 | Cam. Tn. | 18 | C2 |
| Ivybridge La. WC2 | Char. X | 22 | C2 |

## J

| | | | |
|---|---|---|---|
| Jacob's Well Ms. W1 | Bond St. | 16 | B1 |
| James St. W1 | Bond St. | 16 | B1 |
| James St. WC2 | Cov. Gdn. | 23 | C3 |
| Jameson St. W8 | Queens. | 14 | A4 |
| Jamestown Rd. NW1 | Cam. Tn. | 18 | B3 |
| Jasper Wk. N1 | Old St. | 53 | B1 |
| Jay Ms. SW7 | High St. Kens. | 36 | D2 |
| Jeffreys St. NW1 | Cam. Tn. | 18 | C2 |
| Jenner Pl. SW13 | Ravens. Pk. | 35 | A4 |
| Jeremiah St. E14 | Can. Wf. | 19 | C1 |
| Jermyn St. SW1 | Picc. Circ. | 56 | B3 |
| Jerome Cres. NW8 | Mary. | 48 | A1 |
| Jerusalem Pas. EC1 | Farr. | 30 | C1 |
| Jervis Ct. W1 | Ox. Circ. | 54 | B3 |
| Jewry St. EC3 | Ald. | 10 | B3 |
| Joan St. SE1 | S'wark | 64 | C2 |

98

| | | | | | | | | |
|---|---|---|---|---|---|---|---|
| Jockey's Flds. WC1 | Chan. La. | 21 | A2 | Kensington Ct. Pl. | High St. Kens. | 36 | C |
| Johanna St. SE1 | Lamb. N. | 41 | B2 | Kensington Gdns. W2 | Nott. Hill Gate | 52 | D3 |
| John Adam St. WC2 | Char. X | 22 | C2 | Kensington Gdns. Sq. W2 | Bays. | 14 | B1 |
| John Carpenter St. EC4 | Black. | 15 | A3 | Kensington Gate W8 | High St. Kens. | 36 | D3 |
| John Fisher St. E1 | Ald. E. | 10 | D4 | Kensington Gore SW7 | High St. Kens. | 36 | D2 |
| John Harrison Way SE10 | N. Green. | 51 | D4 | Kensington High St. W8 | High St. Kens. | 36 | B3 |
| John Islip St. SW1 | Pim. | 57 | C3 | Kensington High St. W14 | High St. Kens. | 36 | A3 |
| John Princes St. W1 | Ox. Circ. | 54 | B2 | Kensington Mall W8 | Queens. | 14 | A4 |
| John St. WC1 | Chan. La. | 21 | A1 | Kensington Palace Gdns. W8 | Queens. | 14 | B4 |
| John's Ms. WC1 | Chan. La. | 21 | A1 | Kensington Pk. Gdns. W11 | Holl. Pk. | 52 | B2 |
| Joiner St. SE1 | London Br. | 45 | B3 | | | | |
| Jonathan St. SE11 | Vaux. | 68 | D1 | Kensington Pk. Rd. W11 | Lad. Gr. | 52 | B1 |
| Jones St. W1 | Bond St. | 16 | C4 | Kensington Pl. W8 | Nott. Hill Gate | 52 | C3 |
| Jubilee Cres. E14 | N. Green. | 51 | A4 | Kensington Rd. SW7 | High St. Kens. | 36 | D2 |
| Judd St. WC1 | King's X | 39 | B4 | Kensington Rd. W8 | High St. Kens. | 36 | C2 |
| Junction Ms. W2 | Edgw. Rd. | 25 | C4 | Kensington Sq. W8 | High St. Kens. | 36 | C2 |
| Junction Pl. W2 | Padd. | 55 | C2 | Kent Pas. NW1 | Mary. | 48 | C1 |
| Juniper Clo., Wem. | Wem Pk. | 72 | B4 | Kent Yd. SW7 | Knights. | 40 | A2 |
| Juniper Cres. NW1 | Chalk Fm. | 18 | A2 | Kentish Bldgs. SE1 | Boro. | 17 | C2 |
| | | | | Kentish Town Rd. NW1 | Cam. Tn. | 18 | B2 |
| **K** | | | | Kentish Town Rd. NW5 | Chalk Fm. | 18 | B1 |
| Kean St. WC2 | Holb. | 37 | C4 | Kenton St. WC1 | Russ. Sq. | 59 | B1 |
| Keats Pl. EC2 | Moor. | 50 | B3 | Kenway Rd. SW5 | Earls Ct. | 24 | C2 |
| Keeley St. WC2 | Holb. | 37 | C4 | Keppel Row SE1 | Boro. | 17 | A1 |
| Kell St. SE1 | El. & Cas. | 26 | B1 | Keppel St. WC1 | Goodge St. | 32 | D2 |
| Kelly St. NW1 | Chalk Fm. | 18 | B1 | Kerbey St. E14 | Can. Wf. | 19 | C1 |
| Kelso Pl. W8 | High St. Kens. | 36 | C2 | Keybridge Ho. SW8 | Vaux. | 68 | C4 |
| Kelson Ho. E14 | N. Green. | 51 | A4 | Keystone Cres. N1 | King's X | 39 | C2 |
| Kemble St. WC2 | Holb. | 37 | C4 | Keyworth St. SE1 | El. & Cas. | 26 | B1 |
| Kemp's Ct. W1 | Ox. Circ. | 54 | D3 | Kiffen St. EC2 | Old St. | 53 | C3 |
| Kempsford Gdns. SW5 | Earls Ct. | 24 | B3 | Kildare Gdns. W2 | Nott. Hill Gate | 52 | C1 |
| Kempsford Rd. SE11 | El. & Cas. | 26 | A4 | Kildare Ter. W2 | Nott. Hill Gate | 52 | C1 |
| Ken Way, Wem. | Wem Pk. | 72 | D1 | Kilkie Ho. SW8 | Vaux. | 68 | C4 |
| Kendal St. W2 | M. Arch | 47 | A2 | Killick St. N1 | King's X | 39 | D1 |
| Kendall Pl. W1 | Baker St. | 11 | C4 | Kilmarsh Rd. W6 | Hamm. | 35 | B2 |
| Kendrick Ms. SW7 | S. Kens. | 63 | B3 | Kimbolton Row SW3 | S. Kens. | 63 | D4 |
| Kendrick Pl. SW7 | Glos. Rd. | 31 | D3 | King Charles St. SW1 | Westmin. | 73 | A2 |
| Kennet Wf. La. EC4 | Mans. Ho. | 46 | C3 | King Edward St. EC1 | St. Paul's | 61 | C2 |
| Kennington La. SE11 | Vaux. | 68 | D2 | King Edward Wk. SE1 | Lamb. N. | 41 | C3 |
| Kennington Rd. SE1 | Lamb. N. | 41 | B3 | King James St. SE1 | S'wark | 64 | D4 |
| Kenrick Pl. W1 | Baker St. | 11 | C4 | King St. EC2 | Mans. Ho. | 46 | C2 |
| Kensington Ch. Ct. W8 | High St. Kens. | 36 | C2 | King St. SW1 | Green Pk. | 34 | D3 |
| Kensington Ch. St. W8 | Queens. | 14 | A4 | King St. WC2 | Leic. Sq. | 43 | C2 |
| Kensington Ch. Wk. W8 | High St. Kens. | 36 | C2 | King William St. EC4 | Mon. | 49 | B3 |
| Kensington Ct. W8 | High St. Kens. | 36 | C2 | | | | |

| | | | |
|---|---|---|---|
| Kingham Clo. W11 | Holl. Pk. | 52 | A4 |
| Kinghorn St. EC1 | Barb. | 13 | C3 |
| Kingly Ct. W1 | Picc. Circ. | 56 | B1 |
| Kingly St. W1 | Ox. Circ. | 54 | C4 |
| Kings Arms Ct. E1 | Ald. E. | 10 | D1 |
| Kings Arms Yd. EC2 | Bank | 12 | B1 |
| Kings Bench St. SE1 | S'wark | 64 | D3 |
| Kings Bench Wk. EC4 | Black. | 15 | A2 |
| Kings Ct., Wem. | Wem Pk. | 72 | C1 |
| King's Cross Bri. N1 | King's X | 39 | C3 |
| King's Cross Rd. WC1 | King's X | 39 | D3 |
| Kings Dr., Wem. | Wem Pk. | 72 | C1 |
| Kings Head Yd. SE1 | London Br. | 45 | A3 |
| King's Ms. WC1 | Chan. La. | 21 | A1 |
| Kings Pl. SE1 | Boro. | 17 | A3 |
| King's Reach Twr. SE1 | S'wark | 64 | B1 |
| King's Scholars' Pas. SW1 | Vic. | 69 | C2 |
| Kingscote St. EC4 | Black. | 15 | B3 |
| Kingsgate, Wem. | Wem Pk. | 72 | D2 |
| Kingsley Ms. W8 | Glos. Rd. | 31 | A1 |
| Kingstown St. NW1 | Cam. Tn. | 18 | A3 |
| Kingsway WC2 | Holb. | 37 | C3 |
| Kingswood Rd., Wem. | Wem Pk. | 72 | B2 |
| Kinnerton Pl. N. SW1 | Knights. | 40 | C2 |
| Kinnerton Pl. S. SW1 | Knights. | 40 | C2 |
| Kinnerton St. SW1 | Hyde Pk. Cor. | 38 | B3 |
| Kinnerton Yd. SW1 | Knights. | 40 | C2 |
| Kinnoul Rd. W6 | Bar. Ct. | 35 | D4 |
| Kipling Est. SE1 | Boro. | 17 | D3 |
| Kipling St. SE1 | Boro. | 17 | D3 |
| Kirby Gro. SE1 | London Br. | 45 | C4 |
| Kirby St. EC1 | Farr. | 30 | B2 |
| Kirkman Pl. W1 | Goodge St. | 32 | C3 |
| Knaresborough Pl. SW5 | Earls Ct. | 24 | C2 |
| Knights Arc. SW1 | Knights. | 40 | B2 |
| Knights Wk. SE11 | El. & Cas. | 26 | A4 |
| Knightsbridge SW1 | Knights. | 40 | C1 |
| Knightsbridge SW7 | Knights. | 40 | A2 |
| Knightsbridge Grn. SW1 | Knights. | 40 | B2 |
| Knivet Rd. SW6 | W. Brom. | 24 | B4 |
| Knox St. W1 | Mary. | 48 | C3 |
| Kynance Ms. SW7 | Glos. Rd. | 31 | A1 |
| Kynance Pl. SW7 | Glos. Rd. | 31 | B1 |

## L

| | | | |
|---|---|---|---|
| Lackington St. EC2 | Moor. | 50 | C2 |
| Ladbroke Gdns. W11 | Holl. Pk. | 52 | B2 |
| Ladbroke Gro. W11 | Lad. Gr. | 52 | A1 |

| | | | |
|---|---|---|---|
| Ladbroke Rd. W11 | Holl. Pk. | 52 | B3 |
| Ladbroke Sq. W11 | Holl. Pk. | 52 | B2 |
| Ladbroke Ter. W11 | Holl. Pk. | 52 | B2 |
| Ladbroke Wk. W11 | Holl. Pk. | 52 | B3 |
| Lakeside Rd. W14 | Olym. | 35 | C1 |
| Lakeside Way, Wem. | Wem Pk. | 72 | B3 |
| Lamb St. E1 | Liv. St. | 44 | D1 |
| Lambeth Hill EC4 | Mans. Ho. | 46 | B3 |
| Lambeth Rd. SE1 | Lamb. N. | 41 | B4 |
| Lamb's Bldgs. EC1 | Moor. | 50 | B1 |
| Lambs Conduit Pas. WC1 | Holb. | 37 | C1 |
| Lamb's Conduit St. WC1 | Russ. Sq. | 59 | D2 |
| Lamb's Pas. EC1 | Moor. | 50 | B2 |
| Lamington St. W6 | Ravens. Pk. | 35 | A2 |
| Lamlash St. SE11 | El. & Cas. | 26 | A3 |
| Lamont Rd. SW10 | W. Brom. | 24 | D4 |
| Lancashire Ct. W1 | Ox. Circ. | 54 | B4 |
| Lancaster Ct. W2 | Lanc. Gate | 42 | A3 |
| Lancaster Gate W2 | Lanc. Gate | 42 | A3 |
| Lancaster Ms. W2 | Lanc. Gate | 42 | A2 |
| Lancaster Pl. WC2 | Temple | 65 | A2 |
| Lancaster Rd. W11 | Lad. Gr. | 52 | A1 |
| Lancaster St. SE1 | S'wark | 64 | D4 |
| Lancaster Ter. W2 | Lanc. Gate | 42 | B2 |
| Lancaster Wk. W2 | Lanc. Gate | 42 | A4 |
| Lancelot Pl. SW7 | Knights. | 40 | B2 |
| Lancing St. NW1 | Euston | 28 | C3 |
| Landon Pl. SW1 | Knights. | 40 | B3 |
| Landons Clo. E14 | Can. Wf. | 19 | D3 |
| Lanesborough Pl. SW1 | Hyde Pk. Cor. | 38 | C2 |
| Langham Pl. W1 | Ox. Circ. | 54 | B1 |
| Langham St. W1 | Ox. Circ. | 54 | B1 |
| Langley Ct. WC2 | Leic. Sq. | 43 | C2 |
| Langley La. SW8 | Vaux. | 68 | C3 |
| Langley St. WC2 | Cov. Gdn. | 23 | B2 |
| Langthorn Ct. EC2 | Bank | 12 | C1 |
| Langton St. SW10 | W. Brom. | 24 | D4 |
| Lansbury Clo. NW10 | Wem Pk. | 72 | D4 |
| Lansbury Est. E14 | Can. Wf. | 19 | C1 |
| Lansbury Gdns. E14 | Can. Wf. | 19 | D1 |
| Lansdowne Cres. W11 | Holl. Pk. | 52 | B2 |
| Lansdowne Pl. SE1 | Boro. | 17 | D4 |
| Lansdowne Ri. W11 | Lad. Gr. | 52 | A2 |
| Lansdowne Rd. W11 | Lad. Gr. | 52 | A2 |
| Lansdowne Row W1 | Green Pk. | 34 | B2 |
| Lansdowne Ter. WC1 | Russ. Sq. | 59 | C2 |
| Lansdowne Wk. W11 | Holl. Pk. | 52 | B3 |
| Lant St. SE1 | Boro. | 17 | A2 |
| Lanterns Ct. E14 | Can. Wf. | 19 | B4 |

| | | | |
|---|---|---|---|
| Lisle St. WC2 | Leic. Sq. | 43 | B2 |
| Lisson St. NW1 | Edgw. Rd. | 25 | C2 |
| Litchfield St. WC2 | Leic. Sq. | 43 | B2 |
| Little Albany St. NW1 | Gt. Port. St. | 33 | C1 |
| Little Argyll St. W1 | Ox. Circ. | 54 | C3 |
| Little Boltons, The SW5 | Earls Ct. | 24 | C3 |
| Little Boltons, The SW10 | Glos. Rd. | 31 | A4 |
| Little Britain EC1 | Barb. | 13 | B3 |
| Little Chester St. SW1 | Vic. | 69 | A1 |
| Little Dean's Yd. SW1 | Westmin. | 73 | B4 |
| Little Dorrit Ct. SE1 | Boro. | 17 | B2 |
| Little Essex St. WC2 | Temple | 65 | C2 |
| Little George St. SW1 | Westmin. | 73 | B3 |
| Little Marlborough St. W1 | Ox. Circ. | 54 | C3 |
| Little New St. EC4 | Chan. La. | 21 | C4 |
| Little Newport St. WC2 | Leic. Sq. | 43 | B2 |
| Little Portland St. W1 | Ox. Circ. | 54 | B2 |
| Little Russell St. WC1 | Tott. Ct. Rd. | 66 | D2 |
| Little St. James's St. SW1 | Green Pk. | 34 | C3 |
| Little Sanctuary SW1 | St. Jam. Pk. | 60 | D2 |
| Little Smith St. SW1 | St. Jam. Pk. | 60 | D3 |
| Little Somerset St. E1 | Ald. | 10 | B3 |
| Little Titchfield St. W1 | Goodge St. | 32 | A3 |
| Little Trinity La. EC4 | Mans. Ho. | 46 | C3 |
| Little Turnstile WC1 | Holb. | 37 | C2 |
| Liverpool St. EC2 | Liv. St. | 44 | B2 |
| Livonia St. W1 | Ox. Circ. | 54 | D3 |
| Lizard St. EC1 | Old St. | 53 | A2 |
| Lloyd's Ave. EC3 | Ald. | 10 | A3 |
| Lochaline St. W6 | Hamm. | 35 | B4 |
| Locksley Est. E14 | Can. Wf. | 19 | A1 |
| Lockyer Est. SE1 | London Br. | 45 | B4 |
| Lockyer St. SE1 | Boro. | 17 | D3 |
| Lodore St. E14 | Can. Wf. | 19 | D1 |
| Logan Ms. W8 | Earls Ct. | 24 | B2 |
| Logan Pl. W8 | Earls Ct. | 24 | B2 |
| Lolesworth Clo. E1 | Ald. E. | 10 | C1 |
| Loman St. SE1 | S'wark | 64 | D3 |
| Lombard Ct. EC3 | Mon. | 49 | B2 |
| Lombard La. EC4 | Black. | 15 | A2 |
| Lombard St. EC3 | Bank | 12 | C2 |
| Lombardy Pl. W2 | Queens. | 14 | B3 |

| | | | |
|---|---|---|---|
| London Bri. EC4 | Mon. | 49 | B4 |
| London Bri. SE1 | London Br. | 45 | B2 |
| London Bri. St. SE1 | London Br. | 45 | B3 |
| London Bri. Wk. SE1 | London Br. | 45 | B2 |
| London Ms. W2 | Padd. | 55 | C3 |
| London Rd. SE1 | Lamb. N. | 41 | D3 |
| London St. EC3 | T. Hill | 67 | B2 |
| London St. W2 | Padd. | 55 | B2 |
| London Wall EC2 | Moor. | 50 | A3 |
| London Wall Bldgs. EC2 | Moor. | 50 | C3 |
| Long Acre WC2 | Leic. Sq. | 43 | C2 |
| Long Ct. WC2 | Leic. Sq. | 43 | B3 |
| Long La. EC1 | Barb. | 13 | B2 |
| Long La. SE1 | Boro. | 17 | C3 |
| Long Yd. WC1 | Russ. Sq. | 59 | D2 |
| Longford St. NW1 | Gt. Port. St. | 33 | C2 |
| Longmoore St. SW1 | Vic. | 69 | C4 |
| Longridge Rd. SW5 | Earls Ct. | 24 | B2 |
| Longville Rd. SE11 | El. & Cas. | 26 | B3 |
| Lonsdale Rd. W11 | Lad. Gr. | 52 | B1 |
| Lorenzo St. WC1 | King's X | 39 | D2 |
| Loris Rd. W6 | Hamm. | 35 | B1 |
| Lothbury EC2 | Bank | 12 | B1 |
| Lovat La. EC3 | Mon. | 49 | C3 |
| Love La. EC2 | St. Paul's | 61 | D2 |
| Lovegrove Wk. E14 | Can. Wf. | 19 | D3 |
| Lovett Way NW10 | Wem Pk. | 72 | D4 |
| Lower Belgrave St. SW1 | Vic. | 69 | A2 |
| Lower Grosvenor Pl. SW1 | Vic. | 69 | A1 |
| Lower James St. W1 | Picc. Circ. | 56 | B1 |
| Lower John St. W1 | Picc. Circ. | 56 | B1 |
| Lower Lea Crossing E14 | N. Green. | 51 | C1 |
| Lower Mall W6 | Ravens. Pk. | 35 | A3 |
| Lower Marsh SE1 | Lamb. N. | 41 | B4 |
| Lower Robert St. WC2 | Char. X | 22 | B4 |
| Lower Sloane St. SW1 | Sloane Sq. | 62 | C3 |
| Lower Thames St. EC3 | Mon. | 49 | B3 |
| Lowndes Clo. SW1 | Sloane Sq. | 62 | D1 |
| Lowndes Pl. SW1 | Sloane Sq. | 62 | C1 |
| Lowndes Sq. SW1 | Knights. | 40 | C2 |
| Lowndes St. SW1 | Knights. | 40 | C3 |
| Loxham St. WC1 | King's X | 39 | C4 |
| Lucan Pl. SW3 | S. Kens. | 63 | D4 |
| Lucerne Ms. W8 | Queens. | 14 | A4 |

| | | | |
|---|---|---|---|
| Ludgate Bdy. EC4 | Black. | 15 | B2 |
| Ludgate Circ. EC4 | Black. | 15 | B2 |
| Ludgate Hill EC4 | Black. | 15 | B2 |
| Ludgate Sq. EC4 | Black. | 15 | C2 |
| Luke St. EC2 | Old St. | 53 | D3 |
| Lumley Ct. WC2 | Char. X | 22 | C4 |
| Lumley St. W1 | Bond St. | 16 | B2 |
| Lurgan Ave. W6 | Bar. Ct. | 35 | C4 |
| Luton St. NW8 | Edgw. Rd. | 25 | B1 |
| Luxborough St. W1 | Baker St. | 11 | C2 |
| Luxemburg Gdns. W6 | Hamm. | 35 | C2 |
| Lyall Ms. SW1 | Sloane Sq. | 62 | C1 |
| Lyall Ms. W. SW1 | Sloane Sq. | 62 | C1 |
| Lyall St. SW1 | Sloane Sq. | 62 | C1 |
| Lygon Pl. SW1 | Vic. | 69 | A2 |
| Lyme St. NW1 | Cam. Tn. | 18 | C2 |
| Lyons Pl. NW8 | Edgw. Rd. | 25 | A1 |
| Lyons Wk. W14 | Bar. Ct. | 35 | D2 |

## M

| | | | |
|---|---|---|---|
| Mabledon Pl. WC1 | Euston | 28 | D3 |
| Macbeth St. W6 | Ravens. Pk. | 35 | A3 |
| Macclesfield St. W1 | Leic. Sq. | 43 | B2 |
| Macfarren Pl. NW1 | Reg. Pk. | 58 | A2 |
| Macklin St. WC2 | Holb. | 37 | B3 |
| Mackworth St. NW1 | Euston | 28 | A2 |
| Maclise Rd. W14 | Olym. | 35 | D1 |
| Maddox St. W1 | Ox. Circ. | 54 | B4 |
| Magdalen Pas. E1 | T. Hill | 67 | D2 |
| Magdalen St. SE1 | London Br. | 45 | C3 |
| Magpie All. EC4 | Black. | 15 | A2 |
| Mahatma Gandhi Ho., Wem. | Wem Pk. | 72 | A4 |
| Maiden La. NW1 | Cam. Tn. | 18 | D2 |
| Maiden La. WC2 | Cov. Gdn. | 23 | C3 |
| Maidstone Bldgs. SE1 | London Br. | 45 | A3 |
| Malabar St. E14 | Can. Wf. | 19 | B4 |
| Malden Cres. NW1 | Chalk Fm. | 18 | A1 |
| Malet Pl. WC1 | Goodge St. | 32 | C1 |
| Malet St. WC1 | Goodge St. | 32 | C1 |
| Mall, The SW1 | St. Jam. Pk. | 60 | B1 |
| Mall Rd. W6 | Ravens. Pk. | 35 | A3 |
| Mallory St. NW8 | Edgw. Rd. | 25 | C1 |
| Mallow St. EC1 | Old St. | 53 | B3 |
| Maltravers St. WC2 | Temple | 65 | B2 |
| Malvern Ct. SW7 | S. Kens. | 63 | C3 |
| Manbre Rd. W6 | Hamm. | 35 | B4 |
| Manchester Ms. W1 | Baker St. | 11 | C4 |
| Manchester Sq. W1 | M. Arch | 47 | D1 |
| Manchester St. W1 | Baker St. | 11 | C4 |
| Manciple St. SE1 | Boro. | 17 | D3 |

| | | | |
|---|---|---|---|
| Mandela St. NW1 | Cam. Tn. | 18 | C3 |
| Mandeville Pl. W1 | Bond St. | 16 | B1 |
| Manette St. W1 | Tott. Ct. Rd. | 66 | C4 |
| Manilla St. E14 | Can. Wf. | 19 | B4 |
| Manley St. NW1 | Cam. Tn. | 18 | A3 |
| Manningtree St. E1 | Ald. E. | 10 | D2 |
| Manor Dr., Wem. | Wem Pk. | 72 | A3 |
| Mansell St. E1 | Ald. E. | 10 | C3 |
| Mansfield Ms. W1 | Reg. Pk. | 58 | B4 |
| Mansfield St. W1 | Reg. Pk. | 58 | B4 |
| Mansion Ho. EC4 | Bank | 12 | B2 |
| Mansion Ho. Pl. EC4 | Bank | 12 | B2 |
| Manson Ms. SW7 | Glos. Rd. | 31 | D3 |
| Manson Pl. SW7 | Glos. Rd. | 31 | D3 |
| Maple Pl. W1 | Warr. St. | 70 | C3 |
| Maple St. W1 | Goodge St. | 32 | A2 |
| Marble Arch W1 | M. Arch | 47 | B3 |
| Marchbank Rd. W14 | W. Kens. | 24 | A4 |
| Marchmont St. WC1 | Russ. Sq. | 59 | B1 |
| Marco Rd. W6 | Ravens. Pk. | 35 | A1 |
| Margaret Ct. W1 | Ox. Circ. | 54 | C2 |
| Margaret St. W1 | Ox. Circ. | 54 | B2 |
| Margravine Gdns. W6 | Bar. Ct. | 35 | C3 |
| Margravine Rd. W6 | Bar. Ct. | 35 | C3 |
| Marigold All. SE1 | Black. | 15 | B4 |
| Mark La. EC3 | T. Hill | 67 | B2 |
| Mark St. EC2 | Old St. | 53 | D3 |
| Market Ct. W1 | Ox. Circ. | 54 | C2 |
| Market Ms. W1 | Green Pk. | 34 | C2 |
| Market Pl. W1 | Ox. Circ. | 54 | C2 |
| Markham Pl. SW3 | Sloane Sq. | 62 | A4 |
| Markham Sq. SW3 | Sloane Sq. | 62 | A4 |
| Marlborough Clo. SE17 | El. & Cas. | 26 | C4 |
| Marlborough Ct. W8 | Earls Ct. | 24 | B2 |
| Marlborough Gate Ho. W2 | Lanc. Gate | 42 | B2 |
| Marlborough Rd. SW1 | Green Pk. | 34 | D3 |
| Marlborough St. SW3 | S. Kens. | 63 | D4 |
| Marloes Rd. W8 | High St. Kens. | 36 | C3 |
| Marquis Rd. NW1 | Cam. Tn. | 18 | D1 |
| Marsden St. NW5 | Chalk Fm. | 18 | A1 |
| Marsh Wall E14 | Can. Wf. | 19 | B3 |
| Marshall St. W1 | Ox. Circ. | 54 | D3 |
| Marshalsea Rd. SE1 | Boro. | 17 | B2 |
| Marsham St. SW1 | St. Jam. Pk. | 60 | D4 |
| Marshfield St. E14 | N. Green. | 51 | A4 |
| Mart St. WC2 | Cov. Gdn. | 23 | C3 |
| Martin La. EC4 | Mon. | 49 | B2 |
| Martlett Ct. WC2 | Cov. Gdn. | 23 | C2 |
| Mary Pl. W11 | Lad. Gr. | 52 | A2 |

| Name | Area | Ref |
|---|---|---|
| Marylebone Flyover NW1 | Edgw. Rd. | 25 C3 |
| Marylebone Flyover W2 | Edgw. Rd. | 25 B3 |
| Marylebone High St. W1 | Reg. Pk. | 58 A3 |
| Marylebone La. W1 | Reg. Pk. | 58 A4 |
| Marylebone Ms. W1 | Reg. Pk. | 58 B4 |
| Marylebone Pas. W1 | Ox. Circ. | 54 D2 |
| Marylebone Rd. (W) NW1 | Edgw. Rd. | 25 C2 |
| Marylebone Rd. (Cen) NW1 | Baker St. | 11 B3 |
| Marylebone Rd. (E) NW1 | Reg. Pk. | 58 A2 |
| Marylebone St. W1 | Reg. Pk. | 58 A4 |
| Masbro Rd. W14 | Olym. | 35 C1 |
| Masons Arms Ms. W1 | Ox. Circ. | 54 B4 |
| Masons Ave. EC2 | Bank | 12 B1 |
| Mason's Yd. SW1 | Picc. Circ. | 56 B3 |
| Mastmaker Rd. E14 | Can. Wf. | 19 B4 |
| Matheson Rd. W14 | W. Kens. | 24 A2 |
| Matthew Parker St. SW1 | St. Jam. Pk. | 60 D2 |
| Matthews Yd. WC2 | Cov. Gdn. | 23 B2 |
| Maunsel St. SW1 | Pim. | 57 B1 |
| Mayfair Pl. W1 | Green Pk. | 34 B2 |
| Mayfields, Wem. | Wem Pk. | 72 B1 |
| Mayfields Clo., Wem. | Wem Pk. | 72 B1 |
| Mays Ct. WC2 | Char. X | 22 B2 |
| McAuley Clo. SE1 | Lamb. N. | 41 B3 |
| McCoid Way SE1 | Boro. | 17 A3 |
| McLeod's Ms. SW7 | Glos. Rd. | 31 A2 |
| Mead Row SE1 | Lamb. N. | 41 B3 |
| Meadow Ms. SW8 | Vaux. | 68 D4 |
| Meadow Rd. SW8 | Vaux. | 68 D4 |
| Meadow Row SE1 | El. & Cas. | 26 C2 |
| Meard St. W1 | Tott. Ct. Rd. | 66 B4 |
| Mecklenburgh Pl. WC1 | Russ. Sq. | 59 D1 |
| Mecklenburgh Sq. WC1 | Russ. Sq. | 59 D1 |
| Mecklenburgh St. WC1 | Russ. Sq. | 59 D1 |
| Medburn St. NW1 | Morn. Cres. | 18 D4 |
| Medway St. SW1 | St. Jam. Pk. | 60 D4 |
| Melbourne Pl. WC2 | Temple | 65 B1 |
| Melbury Ct. W8 | High St. Kens. | 36 A3 |
| Melbury Rd. W14 | High St. Kens. | 36 A3 |
| Melbury Ter. NW1 | Mary. | 48 B2 |
| Melcombe Pl. NW1 | Mary. | 48 C3 |
| Melcombe St. NW1 | Baker St. | 11 B2 |
| Melior Pl. SE1 | London Br. | 45 C4 |
| Melior St. SE1 | London Br. | 45 C4 |
| Melrose Gdns. W6 | Hamm. | 35 B1 |
| Melton Ct. SW7 | S. Kens. | 63 C4 |
| Melton St. NW1 | Euston Sq. | 29 B2 |
| Memel Ct. EC1 | Barb. | 13 C1 |
| Memel St. EC1 | Barb. | 13 C1 |
| Mepham St. SE1 | Water. | 71 C2 |
| Mercer St. WC2 | Cov. Gdn. | 23 B2 |
| Mercers Pl. W6 | Hamm. | 35 B2 |
| Meridian Gate E14 | Can. Wf. | 19 D4 |
| Mermaid Ct. SE1 | Boro. | 17 C2 |
| Mermaid Ct. SE16 | Can. Wf. | 19 A3 |
| Merrick Sq. SE1 | Boro. | 17 C4 |
| Merrington Rd. SW6 | W. Brom. | 24 B4 |
| Merthyr Ter. SW13 | Ravens. Pk. | 35 A4 |
| Meymott St. SE1 | S'wark | 64 C2 |
| Micawber St. N1 | Old St. | 53 A1 |
| Micklethwaite Rd. SW6 | W. Brom. | 24 B4 |
| Middle St. EC1 | Barb. | 13 C2 |
| Middle Temple EC4 | Temple | 65 C2 |
| Middle Temple La. EC4 | Temple | 65 C1 |
| Middle Yd. SE1 | London Br. | 45 C2 |
| Middlesex Pas. EC1 | Barb. | 13 B3 |
| Middlesex St. E1 | Liv. St. | 44 C2 |
| Middleton Bldgs. W1 | Goodge St. | 32 A3 |
| Midford Pl. W1 | Warr. St. | 70 C3 |
| Midhope St. WC1 | King's X | 39 C4 |
| Midland Rd. NW1 | King's X | 39 A2 |
| Milborne Gro. SW10 | Earls Ct. | 24 D3 |
| Milcote St. SE1 | S'wark | 64 C4 |
| Miles Pl. NW1 | Edgw. Rd. | 25 C2 |
| Miles St. SW8 | Vaux. | 68 B4 |
| Milford La. WC2 | Temple | 65 C2 |
| Milk St. EC2 | St. Paul's | 61 D2 |
| Mill St. W1 | Ox. Circ. | 54 C4 |
| Mill Yd. E1 | Ald. E. | 10 D4 |
| Millbank SW1 | Westmin. | 73 B4 |
| Millbank Twr. SW1 | Pim. | 57 D2 |
| Millennium Way SE10 | N. Green. | 51 C3 |
| Miller St. NW1 | Morn. Cres. | 18 C4 |
| Miller Wk. SE1 | S'wark | 64 B2 |
| Milligan St. E14 | Can. Wf. | 19 A2 |
| Millman Ms. WC1 | Russ. Sq. | 59 D2 |
| Millman St. WC1 | Russ. Sq. | 59 D2 |
| Mills Ct. EC2 | Old St. | 53 D3 |
| Milner St. SW3 | Sloane Sq. | 62 A2 |
| Milroy Wk. SE1 | S'wark | 64 C1 |

| | | | | | | | | |
|---|---|---|---|---|---|---|---|
| Milson Rd. W14 | Olym. | 35 | C1 | Mora St. EC1 | Old St. | 53 | A2 |
| Milton Ct. EC2 | Moor. | 50 | B2 | Morant St. E14 | Can. Wf. | 19 | B2 |
| Milton St. EC2 | Moor. | 50 | B2 | Morden Wf. Rd. SE10 | N. Green. | 51 | C4 |
| Mincing La. EC3 | Mon. | 49 | C2 | More Clo. W14 | Hamm. | 35 | C2 |
| Minera Ms. SW1 | Sloane Sq. | 62 | D2 | Morecambe St. SE17 | El. & Cas. | 26 | D4 |
| Ming St. E14 | Can. Wf. | 19 | B2 | Moreton Pl. SW1 | Pim. | 57 | A3 |
| Minories EC3 | Ald. | 10 | B3 | Moreton St. SW1 | Pim. | 57 | A3 |
| Mint St. SE1 | Boro. | 17 | A2 | Moreton Ter. SW1 | Pim. | 57 | A3 |
| Mitali Pas. E1 | Ald. E. | 10 | D3 | Moreton Ter. Ms. N. SW1 | Pim. | 57 | A3 |
| Mitre Ct. EC2 | St. Paul's | 61 | D2 | | | | |
| Mitre Ct. EC4 | Black. | 15 | A2 | Moreton Ter. Ms. S. SW1 | Pim. | 57 | A3 |
| Mitre Rd. SE1 | S'wark | 64 | B3 | | | | |
| Mitre Sq. EC3 | Ald. | 10 | A3 | Morgans La. SE1 | London Br. | 45 | C3 |
| Mitre St. EC3 | Ald. | 10 | A3 | Morley St. SE1 | Lamb. N. | 41 | C3 |
| Moiety Rd. E14 | Can. Wf. | 19 | B4 | Mornington Ave. W14 | W. Kens. | 24 | A2 |
| Molyneux St. W1 | Edgw. Rd. | 25 | D3 | | | | |
| Monck St. SW1 | St. Jam. Pk. | 60 | D1 | Mornington Cres. NW1 | Morn. Cres. | 18 | C4 |
| Monkwell Sq. EC2 | Moor. | 50 | A3 | | | | |
| Monmouth Pl. W2 | Bays. | 14 | B1 | Mornington St. NW1 | Morn. Cres. | 18 | B4 |
| Monmouth Rd. W2 | Bays. | 14 | A1 | Mornington Ter. NW1 | Morn. Cres. | 18 | B4 |
| Monmouth St. WC2 | Leic. Sq. | 43 | C2 | Morpeth Ter. SW1 | Vic. | 69 | C2 |
| Montagu Mans. W1 | Baker St. | 11 | B3 | Mortimer Mkt. WC1 | Warr. St. | 70 | C3 |
| Montagu Ms. N. W1 | Baker St. | 11 | B4 | Mortimer St. W1 | Ox. Circ. | 54 | C2 |
| Montagu Ms. S. W1 | M. Arch | 47 | C1 | Morton Pl. SE1 | Lamb. N. | 41 | B4 |
| Montagu Ms. W. W1 | M. Arch | 47 | C1 | Morwell St. WC1 | Tott. Ct. Rd. | 66 | C2 |
| Montagu Pl. W1 | Mary. | 48 | C4 | Moscow Pl. W2 | Bays. | 14 | B2 |
| Montagu Row W1 | Baker St. | 11 | B4 | Moscow Rd. W2 | Bays. | 14 | B2 |
| Montagu Sq. W1 | Baker St. | 11 | B4 | Mostyn Ave., Wem. | Wem Pk. | 72 | A4 |
| Montagu St. W1 | M. Arch | 47 | C1 | Motcomb St. SW1 | Knights. | 40 | C3 |
| Montague Clo. SE1 | London Br. | 45 | A2 | Mount, The, Wem. | Wem Pk. | 72 | C1 |
| Montague Pl. WC1 | Goodge St. | 32 | D2 | Mount Dr., Wem. | Wem Pk. | 72 | D1 |
| Montague St. EC1 | Barb. | 13 | C3 | Mount Pleasant WC1 | Chan. La. | 21 | B1 |
| Montague St. WC1 | Russ. Sq. | 59 | B3 | Mount Row W1 | Bond St. | 16 | C4 |
| Monthope Rd. E1 | Ald. E. | 10 | D1 | Mount St. W1 | M. Arch | 47 | D4 |
| Montpelier Ms. SW7 | Knights. | 40 | A3 | Mountague Pl. E14 | Can. Wf. | 19 | D2 |
| Montpelier Pl. SW7 | Knights. | 40 | A3 | Mountford St. E1 | Ald. E. | 10 | D2 |
| Montpelier Sq. SW7 | Knights. | 40 | A3 | Moxon St. W1 | Baker St. | 11 | C4 |
| Montpelier St. SW7 | Knights. | 40 | A2 | Moylan Rd. W6 | Bar. Ct. | 35 | D4 |
| Montpelier Ter. SW7 | Knights. | 40 | A2 | Mozart Ter. SW1 | Sloane Sq. | 62 | D3 |
| Montpelier Wk. SW7 | S. Kens. | 63 | D1 | Mulberry St. E1 | Ald. E. | 10 | D2 |
| Montreal Pl. WC2 | Temple | 65 | A2 | Mulgrave Rd. SW6 | W. Kens. | 24 | A4 |
| Montrose Pl. SW1 | Hyde Pk. Cor. | 38 | C3 | Mulready St. NW8 | Edgw. Rd. | 25 | C1 |
| Monument St. EC3 | Mon. | 49 | B2 | Mulvaney Way SE1 | Boro. | 17 | D3 |
| Moor La. EC2 | Moor. | 50 | B3 | Mumford Ct. EC2 | St. Paul's | 61 | D2 |
| Moor Pl. EC2 | Moor. | 50 | B3 | Mund St. W14 | W. Kens. | 24 | A3 |
| Moor St. W1 | Tott. Ct. Rd. | 66 | C4 | Munden St. W14 | Bar. Ct. | 35 | D2 |
| Moore St. SW3 | Sloane Sq. | 62 | A2 | Munster Sq. NW1 | Gt. Port. St. | 33 | C1 |
| Moorfields EC2 | Moor. | 50 | B3 | Munton Rd. SE17 | El. & Cas. | 26 | D3 |
| Moorgate EC2 | Moor. | 50 | B3 | Murphy St. SE1 | Lamb. N. | 41 | B2 |
| Moorgate Pl. EC2 | Bank | 12 | B1 | Murray Ms. NW1 | Cam. Tn. | 18 | D2 |
| Moorhouse Rd. W2 | Nott. Hill Gate | 52 | C1 | Murray St. NW1 | Cam. Tn. | 18 | D2 |

| | | | |
|---|---|---|---|
| Musard Rd. W6 | Bar. Ct. | 35 | D4 |
| Musard Rd. W14 | Bar. Ct. | 35 | D4 |
| Muscal W6 | Bar. Ct. | 35 | D4 |
| Muscovy St. EC3 | T. Hill | 67 | B3 |
| Museum La. SW7 | S. Kens. | 63 | C2 |
| Museum St. WC1 | Tott. Ct. Rd. | 66 | D2 |

## N

| | | | |
|---|---|---|---|
| Nag's Head Ct. EC1 | Barb. | 13 | D1 |
| Nankin St. E14 | Can. Wf. | 19 | B1 |
| Nantes Pas. E1 | Liv. St. | 44 | D1 |
| Napier Pl. W14 | High St. Kens. | 36 | A3 |
| Napier Rd. W14 | Olym. | 35 | D1 |
| Nasmyth St. W6 | Ravens. Pk. | 35 | A1 |
| Nassau St. W1 | Goodge St. | 32 | A3 |
| Nathaniel Clo. E1 | Ald. E. | 10 | C1 |
| Naval Row E14 | Can. Wf. | 19 | D2 |
| Neal St. WC2 | Cov. Gdn. | 23 | B2 |
| Neal's Yd. WC2 | Cov. Gdn. | 23 | B2 |
| Neathouse Pl. SW1 | Vic. | 69 | C3 |
| Nebraska St. SE1 | Boro. | 17 | C3 |
| Neeld Cres., Wem. | Wem Pk. | 72 | B4 |
| Nella Rd. W6 | Bar. Ct. | 35 | C4 |
| Nelson Pas. EC1 | Old St. | 53 | A2 |
| Nelson Sq. SE1 | S'wark | 64 | C3 |
| Netherton Gro. SW10 | W. Brom. | 24 | D4 |
| Netherwood Rd. W14 | Olym. | 35 | C1 |
| Netley St. NW1 | Euston Sq. | 29 | A2 |
| Nevern Pl. SW5 | Earls Ct. | 24 | B2 |
| Nevern Rd. SW5 | Earls Ct. | 24 | B2 |
| Nevern Sq. SW5 | Earls Ct. | 24 | B2 |
| Neville Clo. NW1 | King's X | 39 | A2 |
| Neville St. SW7 | Glos. Rd. | 31 | D4 |
| Neville Ter. SW7 | Glos. Rd. | 31 | D4 |
| New Bond St. W1 | Bond St. | 16 | C2 |
| New Bri. St. EC4 | Black. | 15 | B2 |
| New Broad St. EC2 | Liv. St. | 44 | B2 |
| New Burlington Ms. W1 | Ox. Circ. | 54 | C4 |
| New Burlington Pl. W1 | Ox. Circ. | 54 | C4 |
| New Burlington St. W1 | Ox. Circ. | 54 | C4 |
| New Cavendish St. W1 | Reg. Pk. | 58 | A4 |
| New Change EC4 | St. Paul's | 61 | C3 |
| New Compton St. WC2 | Tott. Ct. Rd. | 66 | C4 |
| New Ct. EC4 | Temple | 65 | C2 |
| New Coventry St. W1 | Leic. Sq. | 43 | B3 |
| New Fetter La. EC4 | Chan. La. | 21 | C2 |

| | | | |
|---|---|---|---|
| New Goulston St. E1 | Ald. | 10 | B2 |
| New Inn Pas. WC2 | Temple | 65 | B1 |
| New Kent Rd. SE1 | El. & Cas. | 26 | C2 |
| New London St. EC3 | T. Hill | 67 | B2 |
| New N. Pl. EC2 | Old St. | 53 | D4 |
| New N. St. WC1 | Holb. | 37 | C1 |
| New Oxford St. WC1 | Tott. Ct. Rd. | 66 | C3 |
| New Quebec St. W1 | M. Arch | 47 | C2 |
| New Row WC2 | Leic. Sq. | 43 | C2 |
| New Spring Gdns. Wk. SE11 | Vaux. | 68 | C2 |
| New Sq. WC2 | Holb. | 37 | D3 |
| New St. EC2 | Liv. St. | 44 | C2 |
| New St. Sq. EC4 | Chan. La. | 21 | C4 |
| New Turnstile WC1 | Holb. | 37 | C2 |
| New Union Clo. E14 | N. Green. | 51 | A4 |
| New Union St. EC2 | Moor. | 50 | B3 |
| New Wf. Rd. N1 | King's X | 39 | C1 |
| Newburgh St. W1 | Ox. Circ. | 54 | C3 |
| Newbury St. EC1 | Barb. | 13 | C2 |
| Newby Pl. E14 | Can. Wf. | 19 | D2 |
| Newcastle Clo. EC4 | Black. | 15 | B1 |
| Newcastle Pl. W2 | Edgw. Rd. | 25 | C3 |
| Newcastle Row EC1 | Farr. | 30 | B1 |
| Newcombe St. W8 | Queens. | 14 | A4 |
| Newcomen St. SE1 | Boro. | 17 | C2 |
| Newell St. E14 | Can. Wf. | 19 | A1 |
| Newgate St. EC1 | St. Paul's | 61 | B2 |
| Newington Butts SE1 | El. & Cas. | 26 | B4 |
| Newington Butts SE11 | El. & Cas. | 26 | B4 |
| Newington Causeway SE1 | El. & Cas. | 26 | B2 |
| Newman Pas. W1 | Goodge St. | 32 | B3 |
| Newman St. W1 | Goodge St. | 32 | B3 |
| Newman Yd. W1 | Ox. Circ. | 54 | C3 |
| Newman's Ct. EC3 | Bank | 12 | C2 |
| Newman's Row WC2 | Chan. La. | 21 | A3 |
| Newnham Ter. SE1 | Lamb. N. | 41 | B3 |
| Newport Ct. WC2 | Leic. Sq. | 43 | B2 |
| Newport Pl. WC2 | Leic. Sq. | 43 | B2 |
| Newton Rd. W2 | Bays. | 14 | A1 |
| Newton St. WC2 | Holb. | 37 | B3 |
| Nicholas La. EC4 | Mon. | 49 | B2 |
| Nicholson St. SE1 | S'wark | 64 | C2 |
| Nile St. N1 | Old St. | 53 | A1 |
| Noble St. EC2 | St. Paul's | 61 | C2 |
| Noel St. W1 | Ox. Circ. | 54 | D3 |
| Norbiton Rd. E14 | Can. Wf. | 19 | A1 |
| Norfolk Cres. W2 | Edgw. Rd. | 25 | C4 |
| Norfolk Pl. W2 | Padd. | 55 | C2 |
| Norfolk Sq. W2 | Padd. | 55 | C3 |

| | | | |
|---|---|---|---|
| Norfolk Sq. Ms. W2 | Padd. | 55 | C3 |
| Norland Pl. W11 | Holl. Pk. | 52 | A3 |
| Norland Sq. W11 | Holl. Pk. | 52 | A3 |
| Normand Rd. W14 | W. Kens. | 24 | A4 |
| Norris St. SW1 | Picc. Circ. | 56 | C2 |
| North Audley St. W1 | M. Arch | 47 | D2 |
| North Carriage Dr. W2 | Lanc. Gate | 42 | D2 |
| North Colonnade E14 | Can. Wf. | 19 | B3 |
| North Ct. W1 | Goodge St. | 32 | B2 |
| North Cres. WC1 | Goodge St. | 32 | C2 |
| North End Cres. W14 | W. Kens. | 24 | A2 |
| North End Ho. W14 | Bar. Ct. | 35 | D2 |
| North End Rd. SW6 | W. Kens. | 24 | A4 |
| North End Rd. W14 | Bar. Ct. | 35 | D2 |
| North End Rd., Wem. | Wem Pk. | 72 | B2 |
| North Gower St. NW1 | Euston Sq. | 29 | B1 |
| North Ms. WC1 | Chan. La. | 21 | A1 |
| North Ride W2 | Lanc. Gate | 42 | D3 |
| North Row W1 | M. Arch | 47 | C3 |
| North Tenter St. E1 | Ald. E. | 10 | C3 |
| North Ter. SW3 | S. Kens. | 63 | D2 |
| North Vil. NW1 | Cam. Tn. | 18 | D1 |
| North Wk. W2 | Queens. | 14 | D3 |
| North Wf. Rd. W2 | Padd. | 55 | B1 |
| Northburgh St. EC1 | Barb. | 13 | B1 |
| Northdown St. N1 | King's X | 39 | C1 |
| Northington St. WC1 | Chan. La. | 21 | A1 |
| Northumberland All. EC3 | Ald. | 10 | A3 |
| Northumberland Ave. WC2 | Char. X | 22 | B3 |
| Northumberland Pl. W2 | Nott. Hill Gate | 52 | C1 |
| Northumberland St. WC2 | Char. X | 22 | B3 |
| Northumbria St. E14 | Can. Wf. | 19 | B1 |
| Norton Folgate E1 | Liv. St. | 44 | C1 |
| Norwich St. EC4 | Chan. La. | 21 | B4 |
| Notting Hill Gate W11 | Nott. Hill Gate | 52 | C3 |
| Nottingham Ct. WC2 | Cov. Gdn. | 23 | B2 |
| Nottingham Pl. W1 | Baker St. | 11 | C2 |
| Nottingham St. W1 | Baker St. | 11 | C3 |
| Nottingham Ter. NW1 | Baker St. | 11 | C2 |
| Nun Ct. EC2 | Bank | 12 | B1 |
| Nutford Pl. W1 | Edgw. Rd. | 25 | D4 |

## O

| | | | |
|---|---|---|---|
| Oak La. E14 | Can. Wf. | 19 | A2 |
| Oakey La. SE1 | Lamb. N. | 41 | B3 |
| Oakfield St. SW10 | W. Brom. | 24 | D4 |

| | | | |
|---|---|---|---|
| Oakington Ave., Wem. | Wem Pk. | 72 | A2 |
| Oakington Manor Dr., Wem. | Wem Pk. | 72 | B4 |
| Oakley Sq. NW1 | Morn. Cres. | 18 | C4 |
| Oakwood Ct. W14 | High St. Kens. | 36 | A3 |
| Oakwood La. W14 | High St. Kens. | 36 | A3 |
| Oat La. EC2 | St. Paul's | 61 | D2 |
| Observatory Gdns. W8 | High St. Kens. | 36 | B2 |
| Octagon Arc. EC2 | Liv. St. | 44 | B2 |
| Odessa St. SE16 | Can. Wf. | 19 | A4 |
| Odhams Wk. WC2 | Cov. Gdn. | 23 | B2 |
| Ogle St. W1 | Goodge St. | 32 | A2 |
| Old Bailey EC4 | Black. | 15 | C2 |
| Old Barrack Yd. SW1 | Hyde Pk. Cor. | 38 | B3 |
| Old Bond St. W1 | Green Pk. | 34 | C1 |
| Old Brewers Yd. WC2 | Cov. Gdn. | 23 | B2 |
| Old Broad St. EC2 | Bank | 12 | C2 |
| Old Brompton Rd. (N) SW7 | S. Kens. | 63 | B4 |
| Old Brompton Rd. (Cen) SW5 | Earls Ct. | 24 | C3 |
| Old Brompton Rd. (Cen) SW7 | Glos. Rd. | 31 | C4 |
| Old Brompton Rd. (S) SW5 | W. Brom. | 24 | B3 |
| Old Bldgs. WC2 | Chan. La. | 21 | B4 |
| Old Burlington St. W1 | Ox. Circ. | 54 | C4 |
| Old Castle St. E1 | Ald. | 10 | B2 |
| Old Cavendish St. W1 | Bond St. | 16 | C1 |
| Old Compton St. W1 | Picc. Circ. | 56 | C1 |
| Old Ct. Pl. W8 | High St. Kens. | 36 | C2 |
| Old Fish St. Hill EC4 | Mans. Ho. | 46 | B3 |
| Old Fleet La. EC4 | Black. | 15 | B1 |
| Old Gloucester St. WC1 | Russ. Sq. | 59 | C3 |
| Old Jewry EC2 | Bank | 12 | B2 |
| Old Marylebone Rd. NW1 | Edgw. Rd. | 25 | D3 |
| Old Montague St. E1 | Ald. E. | 10 | D1 |
| Old N. St. WC1 | Holb. | 37 | C1 |
| Old Palace Yd. SW1 | Westmin. | 73 | B4 |
| Old Pk. La. W1 | Hyde Pk. Cor. | 38 | C1 |
| Old Pye St. SW1 | St. Jam. Pk. | 60 | C3 |
| Old Quebec St. W1 | M. Arch | 47 | C2 |
| Old Queen St. SW1 | St. Jam. Pk. | 60 | D2 |
| Old Seacoal La. EC4 | Black. | 15 | B2 |
| Old Sq. WC2 | Holb. | 37 | D3 |
| Old St. EC1 | Barb. | 13 | C1 |
| Oldbury Pl. W1 | Reg. Pk. | 58 | A3 |
| Olivers Yd. EC1 | Old St. | 53 | C3 |

| | | | |
|---|---|---|---|
| Park Pl. SW1 | Green Pk. | 34 | C3 |
| Park Pl., Wem. | Wem Pk. | 72 | A3 |
| Park Sq. E. NW1 | Reg. Pk. | 58 | B1 |
| Park Sq. Ms. NW1 | Reg. Pk. | 58 | B2 |
| Park Sq. W. NW1 | Reg. Pk. | 58 | B1 |
| Park St. W1 | M. Arch | 47 | D3 |
| Park Village E. NW1 | Morn. Cres. | 18 | B4 |
| Park Village W. NW1 | Morn. Cres. | 18 | B4 |
| Park Wk. SW10 | W. Brom. | 24 | D4 |
| Park W. W2 | Padd. | 55 | C3 |
| Park W. Pl. W2 | Edgw. Rd. | 25 | D4 |
| Parker Ms. WC2 | Holb. | 37 | B3 |
| Parker St. WC2 | Holb. | 37 | B3 |
| Parkway NW1 | Cam. Tn. | 18 | B3 |
| Parliament Sq. SW1 | Westmin. | 73 | B3 |
| Parliament St. SW1 | Westmin. | 73 | B3 |
| Parry St. SW8 | Vaux. | 68 | B3 |
| Parson's Ho. W2 | Edgw. Rd. | 25 | A1 |
| Passing All. EC1 | Farr. | 30 | C1 |
| Passmore St. SW1 | Sloane Sq. | 62 | C3 |
| Pastor St. SE11 | El. & Cas. | 26 | B3 |
| Pater St. W8 | High St. Kens. | 36 | B3 |
| Paternoster Row EC4 | St. Paul's | 61 | C3 |
| Paternoster Sq. EC4 | St. Paul's | 61 | B2 |
| Patshull Rd. NW5 | Cam. Tn. | 18 | C1 |
| Paul St. EC2 | Old St. | 53 | C4 |
| Pavilion Rd. SW1 | Knights. | 40 | C2 |
| Pavilion St. SW1 | Knights. | 40 | C4 |
| Peabody Dws. WC1 | Russ. Sq. | 59 | B1 |
| Peabody Est. EC1 | Barb. | 13 | D1 |
| Peabody Est. SE1 | S'wark | 64 | B2 |
| Peabody Est. W6 | Hamm. | 35 | B3 |
| Peabody Sq. SE1 | S'wark | 64 | C4 |
| Peabody Trust SE1 | Boro. | 17 | A1 |
| Peace Gro., Wem. | Wem Pk. | 72 | C1 |
| Peacock St. SE17 | El. & Cas. | 26 | B4 |
| Peacock Yd. SE17 | El. & Cas. | 26 | B4 |
| Pear Pl. SE1 | Water. | 71 | C3 |
| Pear Tree Ct. EC1 | Farr. | 30 | B1 |
| Pearman St. SE1 | Lamb. N. | 41 | C3 |
| Peel St. W8 | Nott. Hill Gate | 52 | C3 |
| Peerless St. EC1 | Old St. | 53 | B2 |
| Pekin St. E14 | Can. Wf. | 19 | B1 |
| Pelham Cres. SW7 | S. Kens. | 63 | D4 |
| Pelham Pl. SW7 | S. Kens. | 63 | D3 |
| Pelham St. SW7 | S. Kens. | 63 | C3 |
| Pelling St. E14 | Can. Wf. | 19 | B1 |
| Pemberton Row EC4 | Chan. La. | 21 | C4 |
| Pembridge Cres. W11 | Nott. Hill Gate | 52 | C2 |
| Pembridge Gdns. W2 | Nott. Hill Gate | 52 | C2 |

| | | | |
|---|---|---|---|
| Pembridge Ms. W11 | Nott. Hill Gate | 52 | C2 |
| Pembridge Pl. W2 | Bays. | 14 | A2 |
| Pembridge Rd. W11 | Nott. Hill Gate | 52 | C2 |
| Pembridge Sq. W2 | Queens. | 14 | A3 |
| Pembridge Vil. W2 | Queens. | 14 | A3 |
| Pembridge Vil. W11 | Nott. Hill Gate | 52 | C2 |
| Pembroke Clo. SW1 | Hyde Pk. Cor. | 38 | C3 |
| Pembroke Gdns. W8 | W. Kens. | 24 | A2 |
| Pembroke Gdns. Clo. W8 | High St. Kens. | 36 | A3 |
| Pembroke Pl. W8 | High St. Kens. | 36 | B3 |
| Pembroke Rd. W8 | Earls Ct. | 24 | B2 |
| Pembroke Sq. W8 | High St. Kens. | 36 | B3 |
| Pembroke Studios W8 | High St. Kens. | 36 | A3 |
| Pembroke Vil. W8 | Earls Ct. | 24 | B2 |
| Pembroke Wk. W8 | Earls Ct. | 24 | B2 |
| Penfold Pl. NW1 | Edgw. Rd. | 25 | C2 |
| Penfold St. NW1 | Edgw. Rd. | 25 | B1 |
| Penfold St. NW8 | Edgw. Rd. | 25 | B1 |
| Pennant Ms. W8 | Earls Ct. | 24 | C2 |
| Pennyfields E14 | Can. Wf. | 19 | B2 |
| Penryn St. NW1 | Morn. Cres. | 18 | D4 |
| Pentonville Rd. N1 | King's X | 39 | D2 |
| Penywern Rd. SW5 | Earls Ct. | 24 | B3 |
| Penzance Pl. W11 | Holl. Pk. | 52 | A3 |
| Penzance St. W11 | Holl. Pk. | 52 | A3 |
| Pepper St. SE1 | Boro. | 17 | A2 |
| Pepys St. EC3 | T. Hill | 67 | B2 |
| Percy Ms. W1 | Goodge St. | 32 | C3 |
| Percy Pas. W1 | Goodge St. | 32 | B3 |
| Percy St. W1 | Goodge St. | 32 | C3 |
| Perham Rd. W14 | Bar. Ct. | 35 | D3 |
| Perkin's Rents W1 | St. Jam. Pk. | 60 | C3 |
| Perrers Rd. W6 | Ravens. Pk. | 35 | A2 |
| Perrys Pl. W1 | Tott. Ct. Rd. | 66 | B3 |
| Peter St. W1 | Picc. Circ. | 56 | C1 |
| Peters Hill EC4 | St. Paul's | 61 | C3 |
| Peter's La. EC1 | Farr. | 30 | C2 |
| Petersham La. SW7 | High St. Kens. | 36 | D3 |
| Petersham Ms. SW7 | Glos. Rd. | 31 | B1 |
| Petersham Pl. SW7 | High St. Kens. | 36 | D3 |
| Petley Rd. W6 | Hamm. | 35 | B4 |
| Peto Pl. NW1 | Gt. Port. St. | 33 | C2 |
| Petticoat Sq. E1 | Ald. | 10 | B2 |
| Petty France SW1 | St. Jam. Pk. | 60 | B3 |
| Philbeach Gdns. SW5 | Earls Ct. | 24 | B3 |
| Phillimore Gdns. W8 | High St. Kens. | 36 | B2 |
| Phillimore Pl. W8 | High St. Kens. | 36 | B2 |
| Phillimore Wk. W8 | High St. Kens. | 36 | B3 |
| Philpot La. EC3 | Mon. | 49 | C2 |
| Phipp St. EC2 | Old St. | 53 | D3 |

| | | | | | | | | |
|---|---|---|---|---|---|---|---|---|
| Phipp's Ms. SW1 | Vic. | 69 | A2 | Poplar High St. E14 | Can. Wf. | 19 | C2 |
| Phoenix St. WC2 | Tott. Ct. Rd. | 66 | C4 | Poplar Pl. W2 | Bays. | 14 | B2 |
| Piccadilly (N) W1 | Picc. Circ. | 56 | A3 | Poppins Ct. EC4 | Black. | 15 | B2 |
| Piccadilly (Cen) W1 | Green Pk. | 34 | B3 | Porchester Gdns. W2 | Bays. | 14 | C2 |
| Piccadilly (S) W1 | Hyde Pk. Cor. | 38 | D2 | Porchester Gdns. Ms. | Bays. | 14 | C1 |
| Piccadilly Arc. SW1 | Green Pk. | 34 | B3 | W2 | | | |
| Piccadilly Circ. W1 | Picc. Circ. | 56 | C2 | Porchester Pl. W2 | M. Arch | 47 | A2 |
| Piccadilly Pl. W1 | Picc. Circ. | 56 | B2 | Porchester Sq. W2 | Nott. Hill Gate | 52 | D1 |
| Pickering Pl. SW1 | Green Pk. | 34 | D3 | Porchester Ter. W2 | Bays. | 14 | D2 |
| Pickwick St. SE1 | Boro. | 17 | A3 | Porchester Ter. N. | Nott. Hill Gate | 52 | D1 |
| Picton Pl. W1 | Bond St. | 16 | B2 | W2 | | | |
| Pigott St. E14 | Can. Wf. | 19 | B1 | Porlock St. SE1 | London Br. | 45 | B4 |
| Pilgrim St. EC4 | Black. | 15 | B2 | Porten Rd. W14 | Olym. | 35 | D1 |
| Pilgrimage St. SE1 | Boro. | 17 | C3 | Porter St. W1 | Baker St. | 11 | B3 |
| Pimlico Rd. SW1 | Sloane Sq. | 62 | C4 | Portland Ms. W1 | Ox. Circ. | 54 | D3 |
| Pimlico Wk. N1 | Old St. | 53 | D1 | Portland Pl. W1 | Reg. Pk. | 58 | B2 |
| Pindar St. EC2 | Liv. St. | 44 | B1 | Portland Rd. W11 | Lad. Gr. | 52 | A2 |
| Pineapple Ct. SW1 | Vic. | 69 | C1 | Portman Clo. W1 | M. Arch | 47 | C1 |
| Pinefield Clo. E14 | Can. Wf. | 19 | B2 | Portman Gate NW1 | Mary. | 48 | B2 |
| Pitfield Est. N1 | Old St. | 53 | D1 | Portman Ms. S. W1 | M. Arch | 47 | D2 |
| Pitfield St. N1 | Old St. | 53 | D2 | Portman Sq. W1 | M. Arch | 47 | D1 |
| Pitt St. W8 | High St. Kens. | 36 | B2 | Portman St. W1 | M. Arch | 47 | D2 |
| Pitt's Head Ms. W1 | Hyde Pk. Cor. | 38 | C1 | Portobello Rd. W11 | Lad. Gr. | 52 | B1 |
| Pixley St. E14 | Can. Wf. | 19 | A1 | Portpool La. EC1 | Chan. La. | 21 | B2 |
| Plantain Pl. SE1 | Boro. | 17 | C2 | Portsea Ms. W2 | M. Arch | 47 | A2 |
| Platina St. EC2 | Old St. | 53 | C3 | Portsea Pl. W2 | M. Arch | 47 | A2 |
| Platt St. NW1 | Morn. Cres. | 18 | D4 | Portsmouth St. WC2 | Holb. | 37 | C4 |
| Playhouse Yd. EC4 | Black. | 15 | B2 | Portsoken St. E1 | T. Hill | 67 | C2 |
| Plender St. NW1 | Cam. Tn. | 18 | C3 | Portugal St. WC2 | Holb. | 37 | C4 |
| Plevna St. E14 | N. Green. | 51 | A4 | Post Office Ct. EC3 | Bank | 12 | C2 |
| Pleydell St. EC4 | Black. | 15 | A2 | Poultry EC2 | Bank | 12 | B2 |
| Plough Ct. EC3 | Mon. | 49 | B2 | Powis Gdns. W11 | Lad. Gr. | 52 | B1 |
| Plough Pl. EC4 | Chan. La. | 21 | C4 | Powis Pl. WC1 | Russ. Sq. | 59 | C2 |
| Plough St. E1 | Ald. E. | 10 | C2 | Powis Sq. W11 | Lad. Gr. | 52 | B1 |
| Plumtree Ct. EC4 | Black. | 15 | B1 | Powis Ter. W11 | Lad. Gr. | 52 | B1 |
| Plympton Pl. NW8 | Edgw. Rd. | 25 | C1 | Praed Ms. W2 | Padd. | 55 | C2 |
| Plympton St. NW8 | Edgw. Rd. | 25 | C1 | Praed St. W2 | Padd. | 55 | C2 |
| Pocock St. SE1 | S'wark | 64 | C3 | Pratt St. NW1 | Cam. Tn. | 18 | C3 |
| Poland St. W1 | Ox. Circ. | 54 | D2 | Prescot St. E1 | T. Hill | 67 | D2 |
| Pollen St. W1 | Ox. Circ. | 54 | C3 | Prestage Way E14 | Can. Wf. | 19 | D2 |
| Polygon Rd. NW1 | Euston | 28 | C1 | Prestons Rd. E14 | Can. Wf. | 19 | D4 |
| Pomell Way E1 | Ald. E. | 10 | C2 | Priest Ct. EC2 | St. Paul's | 61 | C2 |
| Pond Pl. SW3 | S. Kens. | 63 | D4 | Primrose Hill EC4 | Black. | 15 | A2 |
| Ponsonby Pl. SW1 | Pim. | 57 | C3 | Primrose St. EC2 | Liv. St. | 44 | B1 |
| Ponsonby Ter. SW1 | Pim. | 57 | C3 | Prince Consort Rd. | S. Kens. | 63 | B1 |
| Pont St. SW1 | Knights. | 40 | B4 | SW7 | | | |
| Pont St. Ms. SW1 | Knights. | 40 | B4 | Prince of Wales Pas. | Euston Sq. | 29 | A2 |
| Ponton Rd. SW8 | Vaux. | 68 | A4 | NW1 | | | |
| Pontypool Pl. SE1 | S'wark | 64 | C3 | Prince of Wales Rd. | Chalk Fm. | 18 | A1 |
| Pooles Bldgs. EC1 | Chan. La. | 21 | B1 | NW5 | | | |
| Poplar Gro., Wem. | Wem Pk. | 72 | D2 | Princedale Rd. W11 | Holl. Pk. | 52 | A3 |

| | | | |
|---|---|---|---|
| Railway App. SE1 | London Br. | 45 | B3 |
| Railway St. N1 | King's X | 39 | C2 |
| Rainsford St. W2 | Edgw. Rd. | 25 | C4 |
| Rainville Rd. W6 | Hamm. | 35 | B4 |
| Raleana Rd. E14 | Can. Wf. | 19 | D3 |
| Ramillies Pl. W1 | Ox. Circ. | 54 | C3 |
| Ramillies St. W1 | Ox. Circ. | 54 | C3 |
| Rampayne St. SW1 | Pim. | 57 | B3 |
| Randolph St. NW1 | Cam. Tn. | 18 | C2 |
| Ranelagh Gro. SW1 | Sloane Sq. | 62 | D4 |
| Ranelagh Rd. SW1 | Pim. | 57 | A4 |
| Rannoch Rd. W6 | Hamm. | 35 | B4 |
| Ranston St. NW1 | Edgw. Rd. | 25 | C2 |
| Raphael St. SW7 | Knights. | 40 | B2 |
| Rathbone Pl. W1 | Goodge St. | 32 | C3 |
| Rathbone St. W1 | Goodge St. | 32 | B3 |
| Ravenscourt Pl. W6 | Ravens. Pk. | 35 | A2 |
| Ravenscourt Rd. W6 | Ravens. Pk. | 35 | A2 |
| Ravey St. EC2 | Old St. | 53 | D3 |
| Rawlings St. SW3 | Sloane Sq. | 62 | A2 |
| Ray St. EC1 | Farr. | 30 | B1 |
| Ray St. Bri. EC1 | Farr. | 30 | B1 |
| Raymond Bldgs. WC1 | Chan. La. | 21 | A2 |
| Raynham Rd. W6 | Ravens. Pk. | 35 | A2 |
| Red Lion St. EC4 | Black. | 15 | A2 |
| Red Lion Sq. WC1 | Holb. | 37 | C2 |
| Red Lion St. WC1 | Holb. | 37 | C1 |
| Red Pl. W1 | M. Arch | 47 | D3 |
| Redan Pl. W2 | Bays. | 14 | B1 |
| Redan St. W14 | Olym. | 35 | C1 |
| Redcliffe Gdns. SW5 | Earls Ct. | 24 | C3 |
| Redcliffe Gdns. SW10 | Earls Ct. | 24 | C3 |
| Redcliffe Ms. SW10 | Earls Ct. | 24 | C3 |
| Redcliffe Pl. SW10 | W. Brom. | 24 | D4 |
| Redcliffe Rd. SW10 | Earls Ct. | 24 | D3 |
| Redcliffe Sq. SW10 | Earls Ct. | 24 | C3 |
| Redcliffe St. SW10 | W. Brom. | 24 | C4 |
| Redcross Way SE1 | Boro. | 17 | B2 |
| Rede Pl. W2 | Bays. | 14 | A2 |
| Redfield La. SW5 | Earls Ct. | 24 | B2 |
| Redhill St. NW1 | Morn. Cres. | 18 | B4 |
| Redmore Rd. W6 | Ravens. Pk. | 35 | A2 |
| Reece Ms. SW7 | S. Kens. | 63 | B3 |
| Reeves Ms. W1 | M. Arch | 47 | D4 |
| Regency Pl. SW1 | Pim. | 57 | C1 |
| Regency St. SW1 | Pim. | 57 | C1 |
| Regent Pl. W1 | Picc. Circ. | 56 | B1 |
| Regent Sq. WC1 | King's X | 39 | C4 |
| Regent St. (N) W1 | Ox. Circ. | 54 | B2 |
| Regent St. (S) SW1 | Picc. Circ. | 56 | C2 |
| Regent's Pk. Est. NW1 | Euston Sq. | 29 | A2 |
| Regnart Bldgs. NW1 | Euston Sq. | 29 | B3 |
| Relton Ms. SW7 | Knights. | 40 | A3 |
| Rembrandt Clo. E14 | N. Green. | 51 | B4 |
| Rembrandt Clo. SW1 | Sloane Sq. | 62 | C3 |
| Remnant St. WC2 | Holb. | 37 | C3 |
| Renfrew Rd. SE11 | El. & Cas. | 26 | A3 |
| Rennie St. SE1 | S'wark | 64 | C1 |
| Rex Pl. W1 | Bond St. | 16 | B4 |
| Rhyl St. NW5 | Chalk Fm. | 18 | A1 |
| Ricardo St. E14 | Can. Wf. | 19 | C1 |
| Rich St. E14 | Can. Wf. | 19 | A2 |
| Richardson's Ms. W1 | Warr. St. | 70 | B3 |
| Richbell Pl. WC1 | Holb. | 37 | C2 |
| Richmond Bldgs. W1 | Tott. Ct. Rd. | 66 | B4 |
| Richmond Ms. W1 | Tott. Ct. Rd. | 66 | B4 |
| Richmond Ter. SW1 | Westmin. | 73 | B2 |
| Rickett St. SW6 | W. Brom. | 24 | B4 |
| Ridgmount Gdns. WC1 | Goodge St. | 32 | C2 |
| Ridgmount Pl. WC1 | Goodge St. | 32 | C2 |
| Ridgmount St. WC1 | Goodge St. | 32 | C2 |
| Riding Ho. St. W1 | Ox. Circ. | 54 | B1 |
| Rigden St. E14 | Can. Wf. | 19 | C1 |
| Ring, The W2 | Lanc. Gate | 42 | D2 |
| Risborough St. SE1 | S'wark | 64 | D3 |
| Rising Sun Ct. EC1 | Barb. | 13 | B3 |
| Rita Rd. SW8 | Vaux. | 68 | C4 |
| Rivercourt Rd. W6 | Ravens. Pk. | 35 | A2 |
| Riverside St. SW8 | Vaux. | 68 | A3 |
| Riverside Gdns. W6 | Ravens. Pk. | 35 | A3 |
| Riverside Wk. SE1 | Water. | 71 | B1 |
| Riverview Gdns. SW13 | Ravens. Pk. | 35 | A4 |
| Rivington St. EC2 | Old St. | 53 | D2 |
| Robert Adam St. W1 | M. Arch | 47 | D1 |
| Robert Dashwood Way SE17 | El. & Cas. | 26 | C4 |
| Robert St. NW1 | Gt. Port. St. | 33 | C1 |
| Robert St. WC2 | Char. X | 22 | C2 |
| Roberts Ms. SW1 | Sloane Sq. | 62 | C1 |
| Robin Hood La. E14 | Can. Wf. | 19 | D1 |
| Rochester Ms. NW1 | Cam. Tn. | 18 | C2 |
| Rochester Pl. NW1 | Cam. Tn. | 18 | C1 |
| Rochester Rd. NW1 | Cam. Tn. | 18 | C1 |
| Rochester Row SW1 | Vic. | 69 | D3 |
| Rochester Sq. NW1 | Cam. Tn. | 18 | C2 |
| Rochester St. SW1 | St. Jam. Pk. | 60 | C4 |
| Rochester Ter. NW1 | Cam. Tn. | 18 | C1 |
| Rochester Wk. SE1 | London Br. | 45 | A2 |
| Rockingham Est. SE1 | El. & Cas. | 26 | C2 |
| Rockingham St. SE1 | El. & Cas. | 26 | C2 |

| | | | |
|---|---|---|---|
| dmarton St. W1 | Baker St. | 11 | B4 |
| dney Pl. SE17 | El. & Cas. | 26 | D3 |
| dney Rd. SE17 | El. & Cas. | 26 | D3 |
| offey St. E14 | Can. Wf. | 19 | D4 |
| ger St. WC1 | Chan. La. | 21 | A1 |
| oland Gdns. SW7 | Glos. Rd. | 31 | C4 |
| oland Way SW7 | Glos. Rd. | 31 | C4 |
| olls Bldgs. EC4 | Chan. La. | 21 | B4 |
| olls Pas. EC4 | Chan. La. | 21 | B4 |
| omilly St. W1 | Picc. Circ. | 56 | C1 |
| Romney Ms. W1 | Baker St. | 11 | C3 |
| Rood La. EC3 | Mon. | 49 | C2 |
| Ropemaker St. EC2 | Moor. | 50 | B2 |
| Roscoe St. EC1 | Barb. | 13 | D1 |
| Rose & Crown Ct. EC2 | St. Paul's | 61 | C2 |
| Rose & Crown Yd. SW1 | Picc. Circ. | 56 | B3 |
| Rose St. WC2 | Leic. Sq. | 43 | C2 |
| Rosebery Sq. EC1 | Chan. La. | 21 | B1 |
| Rosedew Rd. W6 | Bar. Ct. | 35 | C4 |
| Rosefield Gdns. E14 | Can. Wf. | 19 | B2 |
| Rosemoor St. SW3 | Sloane Sq. | 62 | A3 |
| Roserton St. E14 | Can. Wf. | 19 | D4 |
| Rosmead Rd. W11 | Lad. Gr. | 52 | A2 |
| Rossendale Way NW1 | Cam. Tn. | 18 | C3 |
| Rossmore Rd. NW1 | Mary. | 48 | B2 |
| Rotary St. SE1 | Lamb. N. | 41 | D3 |
| Rotherham Wk. SE1 | S'wark | 64 | C2 |
| Rotten Row SW1 | Knights. | 40 | A1 |
| Rotten Row SW7 | Knights. | 40 | A1 |
| Rotterdam Dr. E14 | N. Green. | 51 | A4 |
| Roupell St. SE1 | S'wark | 64 | B2 |
| Rousden St. NW1 | Cam. Tn. | 18 | C2 |
| Rowan Rd. W6 | Hamm. | 35 | C2 |
| Roxby Pl. SW6 | W. Brom. | 24 | B4 |
| Royal Arc. W1 | Green Pk. | 34 | C1 |
| Royal Ave. SW3 | Sloane Sq. | 62 | A4 |
| Royal College St. NW1 | Cam. Tn. | 18 | C2 |
| Royal Ex. EC3 | Bank | 12 | C2 |
| Royal Ex. Ave. EC3 | Bank | 12 | C2 |
| Royal Ex. Bldgs. EC3 | Bank | 12 | C2 |
| Royal Mint Ct. EC3 | T. Hill | 67 | D3 |
| Royal Mint Pl. E1 | T. Hill | 67 | D2 |
| Royal Mint St. E1 | T. Hill | 67 | D2 |
| Royal Opera Arc. SW1 | Picc. Circ. | 56 | C3 |
| Royal Route, Wem. | Wem Pk. | 72 | B3 |
| Royal St. SE1 | Lamb. N. | 41 | D4 |
| Royalty Ms. W1 | Tott. Ct. Rd. | 66 | B4 |
| Rudolf Pl. SW8 | Vaux. | 68 | C4 |
| Rufus St. N1 | Old St. | 53 | D2 |
| Rugby St. WC1 | Russ. Sq. | 59 | D2 |
| Rugg St. E14 | Can. Wf. | 19 | B2 |
| Runcorn Pl. W11 | Lad. Gr. | 52 | A2 |
| Rupert Ct. W1 | Picc. Circ. | 56 | C1 |
| Rupert St. W1 | Picc. Circ. | 56 | C1 |
| Rushworth St. SE1 | S'wark | 64 | D3 |
| Russell Ct. SW1 | Green Pk. | 34 | D3 |
| Russell Gdns. W14 | Olym. | 35 | D1 |
| Russell Gdns. Ms. W14 | Holl. Pk. | 52 | A4 |
| Russell Rd. W14 | Olym. | 35 | D1 |
| Russell Sq. WC1 | Russ. Sq. | 59 | B2 |
| Russell St. WC2 | Cov. Gdn. | 23 | C3 |
| Russia Ct. EC2 | Mans. Ho. | 46 | C2 |
| Russia Row EC2 | Mans. Ho. | 46 | C2 |
| Rutherford St. SW1 | Pim. | 57 | B1 |
| Rutherford Way, Wem. | Wem Pk. | 72 | B2 |
| Rutland Gdns. SW7 | Knights. | 40 | A2 |
| Rutland Gdns. Ms. SW7 | Knights. | 40 | A2 |
| Rutland Gate SW7 | Knights. | 40 | A2 |
| Rutland Gro. W6 | Ravens. Pk. | 35 | A3 |
| Rutland Ms. E. SW7 | S. Kens. | 63 | D1 |
| Rutland Ms. S. SW7 | S. Kens. | 63 | D1 |
| Rutland Pl. EC1 | Barb. | 13 | B2 |
| Rutland St. SW7 | Knights. | 40 | A3 |
| Ryder Ct. SW1 | Picc. Circ. | 56 | B3 |
| Ryder St. SW1 | Picc. Circ. | 56 | B3 |
| Ryder Yd. SW1 | Picc. Circ. | 56 | B3 |
| Ryland Rd. NW5 | Chalk Fm. | 18 | B1 |
| Rylston Rd. SW6 | W. Kens. | 24 | A4 |
| Rysbrack St. SW3 | Knights. | 40 | B3 |

## S

| | | | |
|---|---|---|---|
| Sackville St. W1 | Picc. Circ. | 56 | B2 |
| Saffron Ave. E14 | N. Green. | 51 | B1 |
| Saffron Hill EC1 | Farr. | 30 | B2 |
| Saffron St. EC1 | Farr. | 30 | B2 |
| Sage Way WC1 | King's X | 39 | D4 |
| St. Albans Gro. W8 | High St. Kens. | 36 | C3 |
| St. Albans Ms. W2 | Edgw. Rd. | 25 | B2 |
| St. Albans St. SW1 | Picc. Circ. | 56 | C2 |
| St. Alphage Gdns. EC2 | Moor. | 50 | A3 |
| St. Andrew St. EC4 | Chan. La. | 21 | C3 |
| St. Andrew's Hill EC4 | Black. | 15 | C3 |
| St. Andrews Pl. NW1 | Gt. Port. St. | 33 | C2 |
| St. Andrews Rd. W14 | Bar. Ct. | 35 | D4 |
| St. Anne's Ct. W1 | Tott. Ct. Rd. | 66 | B4 |

| | | | |
|---|---|---|---|
| Southcombe St. W14 | Bar. Ct. | 35 | D2 |
| Southern St. N1 | King's X | 39 | D1 |
| Southerton Rd. W6 | Hamm. | 35 | B1 |
| Southwark Bri. EC4 | Mans. Ho. | 46 | C4 |
| Southwark Bri. SE1 | Mans. Ho. | 46 | C4 |
| Southwark Bri. Rd. SE1 | Boro. | 17 | A3 |
| Southwark Gro. SE1 | Boro. | 17 | A1 |
| Southwark St. SE1 | S'wark | 64 | D1 |
| Southwater Clo. E14 | Can. Wf. | 19 | A1 |
| Southwell Gdns. SW7 | Glos. Rd. | 31 | B1 |
| Southwick Ms. W2 | Padd. | 55 | C2 |
| Southwick Pl. W2 | Padd. | 55 | D3 |
| Southwick St. W2 | Edgw. Rd. | 25 | C4 |
| Spanish Pl. W1 | Bond St. | 16 | B3 |
| Spear Ms. SW5 | Earls Ct. | 24 | B2 |
| Speedy Pl. WC1 | King's X | 39 | B4 |
| Spenser St. SW1 | St. Jam. Pk. | 60 | B3 |
| Spital Sq. E1 | Liv. St. | 44 | C1 |
| Spital Yd. E1 | Liv. St. | 44 | C1 |
| Spitalfields Mkt. E1 | Liv. St. | 44 | D1 |
| Sprimont Pl. SW3 | Sloane Sq. | 62 | A4 |
| Spring Gdns. SW1 | Char. X | 22 | A3 |
| Spring Ms. W1 | Baker St. | 11 | B3 |
| Spring St. W2 | Padd. | 55 | B3 |
| Springvale Ter. W14 | Olym. | 35 | C1 |
| Spur Rd. SW1 | St. Jam. Pk. | 60 | A2 |
| Square, The W6 | Hamm. | 35 | B3 |
| Stable Yd. SW1 | Green Pk. | 34 | C4 |
| Stable Yd. Rd. SW1 | St. Jam. Pk. | 60 | B1 |
| Stacey St. WC2 | Tott. Ct. Rd. | 66 | C4 |
| Stackhouse St. SW3 | Knights. | 40 | B3 |
| Stadium Way, Wem. | Wem Pk. | 72 | A3 |
| Staff St. EC1 | Old St. | 53 | C2 |
| Stafford Pl. SW1 | Vic. | 69 | C1 |
| Stafford St. W1 | Green Pk. | 34 | C2 |
| Stafford Ter. W8 | High St. Kens. | 36 | B2 |
| Stag Pl. SW1 | Vic. | 69 | C1 |
| Stainer St. SE1 | London Br. | 45 | B3 |
| Staining La. EC2 | St. Paul's | 61 | D2 |
| Stainsby Pl. E14 | Can. Wf. | 19 | B1 |
| Stainsby Rd. E14 | Can. Wf. | 19 | B1 |
| Stalbridge St. NW1 | Mary. | 48 | B3 |
| Stamford St. SE1 | Water. | 71 | C2 |
| Stanford Rd. W8 | High St. Kens. | 36 | C3 |
| Stanford St. SW1 | Pim. | 57 | B2 |
| Stanhope Gdns. SW7 | Glos. Rd. | 31 | C2 |
| Stanhope Ms. E. SW7 | Glos. Rd. | 31 | C2 |
| Stanhope Ms. S. SW7 | Glos. Rd. | 31 | C3 |
| Stanhope Ms. W. SW7 | Glos. Rd. | 31 | C2 |
| Stanhope Par. NW1 | Euston | 28 | A2 |
| Stanhope Pl. W2 | M. Arch | 47 | B2 |
| Stanhope Row W1 | Green Pk. | 34 | A3 |
| Stanhope St. NW1 | Euston | 28 | A2 |
| Stanhope Ter. W2 | Lanc. Gate | 42 | C2 |
| Stanley Clo. SW8 | Vaux. | 68 | D4 |
| Stanley Cres. W11 | Holl. Pk. | 52 | B2 |
| Stanley Gdns. W11 | Holl. Pk. | 52 | B2 |
| Stanley Pas. NW1 | King's X | 39 | B2 |
| Stanwick Rd. W14 | W. Kens. | 24 | A2 |
| Staple Inn Bldgs. WC1 | Chan. La. | 21 | B3 |
| Staple St. SE1 | Boro. | 17 | D3 |
| Star Pl. E1 | T. Hill | 67 | D3 |
| Star Rd. W14 | W. Kens. | 24 | A4 |
| Star St. W2 | Padd. | 55 | C2 |
| Star Yd. WC2 | Chan. La. | 21 | B4 |
| Starcross St. NW1 | Euston Sq. | 29 | B2 |
| Station App. SE1 | Lamb. N. | 41 | A2 |
| Stedham Pl. WC1 | Tott. Ct. Rd. | 66 | B3 |
| Steedman St. SE17 | El. & Cas. | 26 | C4 |
| Stephen Ms. W1 | Goodge St. | 32 | C3 |
| Stephen St. W1 | Goodge St. | 32 | C3 |
| Stephenson Way NW1 | Euston Sq. | 29 | B3 |
| Sterling St. SW7 | Knights. | 40 | A2 |
| Sterndale Rd. W14 | Olym. | 35 | C1 |
| Sterry St. SE1 | Boro. | 17 | C3 |
| Stew La. EC4 | Mans. Ho. | 46 | B3 |
| Steward St. E1 | Liv. St. | 44 | C1 |
| Stewart St. E14 | Can. Wf. | 19 | D4 |
| Stillington St. SW1 | Vic. | 69 | D3 |
| Stone Bldgs. WC2 | Chan. La. | 21 | A3 |
| Stone Ho. Ct. EC3 | Ald. | 10 | A2 |
| Stonecutter St. EC4 | Black. | 15 | B1 |
| Stones End St. SE1 | Boro. | 17 | A3 |
| Stoney La. E1 | Ald. | 10 | B2 |
| Stoney St. SE1 | London Br. | 45 | A2 |
| Stonor Rd. W14 | W. Kens. | 24 | A2 |
| Store St. WC1 | Goodge St. | 32 | C3 |
| Storey's Gate SW1 | St. Jam. Pk. | 60 | D2 |
| Stourcliffe St. W1 | M. Arch | 47 | B2 |
| Strafford St. E14 | Can. Wf. | 19 | B4 |
| Strand WC2 | Char. X | 22 | B2 |
| Strand La. WC2 | Temple | 65 | B2 |
| Stratford Pl. W1 | Bond St. | 16 | C2 |
| Stratford Rd. W8 | High St. Kens. | 36 | B3 |
| Stratford Vil. NW1 | Cam. Tn. | 18 | C2 |
| Strathearn Pl. W2 | Lanc. Gate | 42 | D2 |
| Strathmore Gdns. W8 | Queens. | 14 | A4 |
| Stratton St. W1 | Green Pk. | 34 | B2 |
| Strattondale St. E14 | N. Green. | 51 | A4 |
| Streatham St. WC1 | Tott. Ct. Rd. | 66 | D3 |

## U

## V

| | | | |
|---|---|---|---|
| Wicklow St. WC1 | King's X | 39 | D3 |
| Widegate St. E1 | Liv. St. | 44 | C2 |
| Wigmore Pl. W1 | Bond St. | 16 | C1 |
| Wigmore St. W1 | M. Arch | 47 | D2 |
| Wilbraham Pl. SW1 | Sloane Sq. | 62 | B2 |
| Wilby Ms. W11 | Holl. Pk. | 52 | B3 |
| Wilcox Pl. SW1 | St. Jam. Pk. | 60 | B4 |
| Wild Ct. WC2 | Holb. | 37 | C3 |
| Wild St. WC2 | Cov. Gdn. | 23 | C2 |
| Wilfred St. SW1 | Vic. | 69 | C1 |
| Wilkin St. NW5 | Chalk Fm. | 18 | B1 |
| Willes Rd. NW5 | Chalk Fm. | 18 | B1 |
| William IV St. WC2 | Char. X | 22 | B2 |
| William Ms. SW1 | Knights. | 40 | C2 |
| William Rd. NW1 | Euston Sq. | 29 | A2 |
| William St. SW1 | Knights. | 40 | C2 |
| Willis St. E14 | Can. Wf. | 19 | C1 |
| Willoughby St. WC1 | Tott. Ct. Rd. | 66 | D2 |
| Willow Ct. EC2 | Old St. | 53 | D3 |
| Willow Pl. SW1 | Vic. | 69 | D3 |
| Willow St. EC2 | Old St. | 53 | D3 |
| Wilmot Pl. NW1 | Cam. Tn. | 18 | C2 |
| Wilson St. EC2 | Moor. | 50 | C2 |
| Wilsons Rd. W6 | Bar. Ct. | 35 | C3 |
| Wilton Cres. SW1 | Hyde Pk. Cor. | 38 | B3 |
| Wilton Ms. SW1 | Hyde Pk. Cor. | 38 | C4 |
| Wilton Pl. SW1 | Hyde Pk. Cor. | 38 | B3 |
| Wilton Rd. SW1 | Vic. | 69 | B2 |
| Wilton Row SW1 | Hyde Pk. Cor. | 38 | B3 |
| Wilton St. SW1 | Vic. | 69 | A1 |
| Wilton Ter. SW1 | Hyde Pk. Cor. | 38 | B4 |
| Wiltshire Clo. SW3 | Sloane Sq. | 62 | A3 |
| Wimpole Ms. W1 | Reg. Pk. | 58 | B3 |
| Wimpole St. W1 | Reg. Pk. | 58 | A4 |
| Winchester Clo. SE17 | El. & Cas. | 26 | B4 |
| Winchester Sq. SE1 | London Br. | 45 | A2 |
| Winchester Wk. SE1 | London Br. | 45 | A2 |
| Windmill St. W1 | Goodge St. | 32 | C3 |
| Windmill Wk. SE1 | S'wark | 64 | B2 |
| Windsor Cres., Wem. | Wem Pk. | 72 | C2 |
| Windsor Pl. SW1 | St. Jam. Pk. | 60 | B4 |
| Windsor Ter. N1 | Old St. | 53 | A1 |
| Windsor Way W14 | Hamm. | 35 | C2 |
| Wine Office Ct. EC4 | Black. | 15 | A2 |
| Wingate Rd. W6 | Ravens. Pk. | 35 | A1 |
| Wingrave Rd. W6 | Hamm. | 35 | B4 |
| Winnett St. W1 | Picc. Circ. | 56 | C1 |
| Winsland Ms. W2 | Padd. | 55 | B2 |
| Winsland St. W2 | Padd. | 55 | B2 |
| Winsley St. W1 | Ox. Circ. | 54 | C2 |
| Winslow Rd. W6 | Hamm. | 35 | B4 |

| | | | |
|---|---|---|---|
| Woburn Pl. WC1 | Russ. Sq. | 59 | A1 |
| Woburn Sq. WC1 | Russ. Sq. | 59 | A2 |
| Woburn Wk. WC1 | Euston | 28 | D3 |
| Wollaston Clo. SE1 | El. & Cas. | 26 | C3 |
| Wolsey Ms. NW5 | Cam. Tn. | 18 | C1 |
| Wolverton Gdns. W6 | Hamm. | 35 | C2 |
| Wood St. EC2 | Mans. Ho. | 46 | C2 |
| Woods Ms. W1 | M. Arch | 47 | D3 |
| Woodsford Sq. W14 | Holl. Pk. | 52 | A4 |
| Woodstock Ms. W1 | Reg. Pk. | 58 | A4 |
| Woodstock St. W1 | Bond St. | 16 | C2 |
| Woodstock Ter. E14 | Can. Wf. | 19 | C2 |
| Woolmore St. E14 | Can. Wf. | 19 | D2 |
| Wootton St. SE1 | S'wark | 64 | B2 |
| Worgan St. SE11 | Vaux. | 68 | D1 |
| Worlidge St. W6 | Hamm. | 35 | B3 |
| Wormwood St. EC2 | Liv. St. | 44 | B3 |
| Worship St. EC2 | Old St. | 53 | C4 |
| Wrights La. W8 | High St. Kens. | 36 | C3 |
| Wyatt Clo. SE16 | Can. Wf. | 19 | A4 |
| Wyatt Dr. SW13 | Ravens. Pk. | 35 | A4 |
| Wyndham Ms. W1 | Mary. | 48 | C4 |
| Wyndham Pl. W1 | Mary. | 48 | C4 |
| Wyndham St. W1 | Mary. | 48 | C3 |
| Wyndham Yd. W1 | Mary. | 48 | C4 |
| Wynford Rd. N1 | King's X | 39 | D1 |
| Wynnstay Gdns. W8 | High St. Kens. | 36 | B3 |
| Wythburn Pl. W1 | M. Arch | 47 | B2 |
| Wyvil Rd. SW8 | Vaux. | 68 | B4 |

**Y**

| | | | |
|---|---|---|---|
| Yabsley St. E14 | Can. Wf. | 19 | D3 |
| Yarmouth Pl. W1 | Green Pk. | 34 | A3 |
| Yeldham Rd. W6 | Bar. Ct. | 35 | C3 |
| Yeoman's Row SW3 | Knights. | 40 | A4 |
| Yeomans Yd. E1 | T. Hill | 67 | D2 |
| York Bri. NW1 | Baker St. | 11 | C1 |
| York Bldgs. WC2 | Char. X | 22 | C2 |
| York Gate NW1 | Baker St. | 11 | C2 |
| York Ho., Wem. | Wem Pk. | 72 | A3 |
| York Ho. Pl. W8 | High St. Kens. | 36 | C2 |
| York Pl. WC2 | Char. X | 22 | C2 |
| York Rd. SE1 | Water. | 71 | B3 |
| York St. W1 | Mary. | 48 | C4 |
| York Ter. E. NW1 | Reg. Pk. | 58 | A2 |
| York Ter. W. NW1 | Baker St. | 11 | C2 |
| York Way N7 | Cam. Tn. | 18 | D1 |
| Yorkshire Grey Yd. WC1 | Holb. | 37 | C2 |
| Young St. W8 | High St. Kens. | 36 | C2 |
| Young's Bldgs. EC1 | Old St. | 53 | A3 |

# Index to Places of Interest